One Soul

Gerald A. Gott

To: Dimaree

From: Jerry

God Bless

Silkhaven Publishing, LLC
ISBN: 978-0-9981866-8-9 (ebook)

ISBN: 978-0-9981866-9-6 (paperback)

Library of Congress Control Number: 2016961166

Copyright (c) 2016, Gerald A. Gott

(V1) – December 15, 2016

DEDICATION

I dedicate this book of poems to my wife, Sandy, and to our children and grandchildren. These poems are an accumulation of poems I have written through the years of my life.

These are words I could not say aloud due to fear of rejection. I feel very comfortable putting them down on paper. I think of myself as a depressive type of writer. I also think this is a gift which my Lord has given me. A gift that should be shared with others.

My hope is that some of the poetry within these pages will relate to you, the reader. This is one of the reasons I wrote the book. May our Lord bless each and every one of you.

Table of Contents

Dearest One

Thy Love is Mine

Lonely Hearts

My Love

Once Again

Tears in the Rain

Silent Love

My Love

Thy Love is Mine

Lost Moments

Touch Me Not

Lonely Mist

Fadded Memories

Forgotten Times

Heart Strings

Brothers

Love Upon the Rocks

Loneliness - Page 63

Stillness of Life

Searching

Leaving

Outcast

Alone

Silent Falls

Darken Cell

Shattered Dreams

Whispers in the Wind

O My Soul

The Book

Spirit's Broken

Torn Within

Whispers Not

Lifeless Souls

Trail of Tears

Mourn

Voices

Broken Tears

Eternal Light

Misty Gray

Along the Road

Tears in the Wind

Time - Page 109

Vapor of Time

Endless Time

Sweet Hour

Tragic

Vast Domain

Silent Eternity

Farewell

Foot Steps

Despair in Time

Denied

Endless Sand

Spiral into Silence

Yesterday

Time Itself

Only Time

Simple Times

Lonely Hour

Present Time

No More

Silent Times

Inner Self and Friendship - Page 130

Serene

Falling Crystals

Silent Tears

From Without

Solitude

Tears upon the Pillow

Taps

Tears upon Stones

Searching

Madness

The Room

Depths of Man

The Group

No Other

The Flag

Quiet Space

Friend

Sorrows

Intruder

Broken Spirits

Shadoiw in the Wind

Eternal Cry

Somewhere in the Night

Silent Sounds

Human Voices

Whispering Winds

Days of Solace

Quiet Moments

Depression

Friends

Lasting Friendship

Nature - Page 162

Rain Drops

Mountain Top

Rustle Among the Trees

In the Shadows

Sun Rise

Silent Greens

Breaking Water

Death of a Flower

Ripples in the Water

Wolves

Ambers of Sun Light

Little Flower

Distance

Eyes of Steel

Heavenly Waters

Sounds of Creation

Before Dawn

Sparrow's Flight

Flower's Adrift

Wintery Wind

Hills of Beauty

Cold Winds

Sunlight

Feathered Friends

Snowflake

Majestic Seas

Within the Clouds

Darkness, Sins, and Evil - Page 190

Only Darkness

Lonely Depths

Asylum

Penitence

Loathe

Flames

Unworthy

The Empty Sill

Darken Walls

Sphere of Darkness

Darken Souls

Inner Darkness

Darkened Mist

Darkness Follows

A Time to Weep

Mercy

Silent Skies

Solemn Hour

Shadow of Evil

Reaper of Sorrow

Evil

Death and the Grave - Page 212

Lonely Tombstone

O' Death

Crystals from Within

Old Soldier

The Granite's Cry

Misconception

Rocks which Hide

The Blue Maze

The Reaper

Distant

Tears Upon the Grave

Silent Fall

Cry of Life

Cry Not

Legacy

Even Moor

Death

Misty Eyes

Death is Near

Ashes Upon Stone

White Stones

Tombstone

About the Author

Other Books by Gerald A. Gott

God and His
Beloved Son

STEPS OF A FOOL

My God and my Lord, I have walked, among the
Fools, and thought that I, was someone new.
I cursed the ground, and breathe the air, and
Never thought, or even cared.

Who is God? Some lofty soul! For I am man,
For man alone, shall rule the earth, and
Conquer space.

O' the lowly souls which cry, for their God,
In darken skies, for there is, no sound from
Empty winds, they seek their God, with empty
Hands.

Who has wisdom, beyond the stars, and
Understanding like ocean's depths, only man
Who takes a step, toward the heaven's, beyond
The skies, for in the future, is where it lies
As God looks down, with broken heart, knowing
Man, shall soon depart, into the depths, of
Hell itself, for man alone, has strayed away,
Walking in the darken path, away from Light,
And on to death.

GERALD A. GOTT
Date unknown

THE SECOND COMING

Flesh melted from bones like candle wax,
Not even a scream came from their lips
As the light took away their lives.

Their bones stood naked for one small moment,
Like eternity itself, then fell like tree limbs
Upon the scorched ground.

The land so barren, with no sign of life,
The cracked ground thirsty for rain drops
Which are no more, the burnt ashes of trees
That once stood tall and majestic as kings
Once did, the sky is empty, for no life exists.

As the wind blows like howling dogs in the night,
Only God alone saw this sight. For He had said
In days of past; "I shall return upon this earth,
And all those living, which have denied me, shall
Know fear from the depths of their souls."

And so the end came with a flash of light,
And darkness stood forever upon the earth.
No sound to be heard, no cries of fear, for
Fear itself has past away, only God knows that faithful day.

GERALD A. GOTT
Before 30 December 1994

THE VOICE

I hear it calling me, a
Voice which only I can hear,
Still calling for me.

I heard this voice, when I
Was young, I knew then, it
Would return.

Again, I hear the voice, I
Turn around, no one there,
The voice abounds.

I fear, and yet, I seek to
Find the voice, which calls
For me. I knew others, who
Heard the voice, and told
No one, but themselves.

Why does the voice call only me?
I have so much, and there is nothing,
Is this why the voice beckon's me?

The voice, it grows stronger as time
Passes by, I wonder why, it has not
Cried.

I hear the voice, my times begun,
The voice I seek, is underground.
Seek me not, for this I know, the
Voice and I, at last are home.

GERALD A. GOTT
10 January 1995

4

ONLY TIME

Only time I have left, no one here,
No sight, no breath. As the clouds pass
Me by, I wander on as if I'm blind.

Why only me? I cry aloud, to fall on
Deaf ears, within these walls. I can't
See the vapors as they pass by, the vapors
Of time, is why I'm blind.

To see the sky, the sun and moon, if
Only I could look at you, for within this
Frame of mine, there's only sadness, which
Now I hide.

For time itself has bound me so, for in time
My tormented soul, shall see no light, within
The skies, for time itself, has made me blind.

GERALD A. GOTT
20 June 1995

TOUCH OF HIS GARMENT

I see the Master beyond the trees,
If only He would see me, before I flee.
The crowd so large, so many which I
Fear, and yet I know within, I must get
Near.

To touch His garment, would make me
Whole, for in my heart, this truth I know.
The crowd is moving, as if by faith, towards
Me on this lonely day.

The crowd's before me, I can hardly see, the
Master's face, which is turned from me. Through
The crowd I stretch my hand, and pray the Lord, I
Touch this man.

He passes by, my hand thrust out, to touch His
Garment, I have no doubt, my body healed,
I cry and shout!

The Master turns, and faces me, with eyes of
Compassion, He speaks to me, for He has made
My body whole, and with my body, He saved my soul.

GERALD A. GOTT
31 July 1995

THE HILL

The hill so far away, I see it through
The sun light's rays, for upon this hilltop's
Crest, my soul and hope will surely rest.

Upon the peak of dirt and grime, my heart
Shall sink, with fear inside. Fear within this
Body's frame, my heart and mind can feel
The pain.

Tied upon the tree of death, my soul and heart
Can find no breath, for death itself shall surely
Come, for I wait, thy will be done.

Upon the hill of no return, my soul aflame, as
Embers burn, as I watch the crowd below, I
Pray my Lord, to save their souls.

As the pain within me screams, I thank my Lord,
For loving me. My blood runs down the wooden
Pine, upon the ground is all they find, stains of blood,
No longer new, because the blood, was shed for you.

I died upon Gol'go-tha's hill, amiss the hate of souls
Gone mad, knowing not the Master's hand. The prophets
Spoke in days of old, for this would happen, upon my soul.

As the priests and scribes come by, I watch them closely,
With my eyes, mocking, jeering, closing in, only hate
Within their hands.

As I hear His cry above, I knew He died because of love,
For in His death, we have life, this I know, because of mine.
My eyes grow tired, my mind is numb, the pain no longer
Consumes my soul, for death's at hand, for this, I know.

GERALD A. GOTT
7 August 1995

BROKEN

Upon this tree from which I hang,
The world below me, has shown
Its shame. The body swollen, from
Bruises within, my words have fallen
On empty winds.

The body broken, for no one sees, the
Soul which hangs upon this tree. The soul
Which cries, Abba Father into the sky, and
Ask, my Father, why is it I?

Through the pain within His eyes, no one
Knows the reason why. Only death is yet
Beyond, which cries aloud, for God's own
Son.

He asks the Father, forgive them all, and no
One sees for whom He called. The sun turns
Dark, and runs with blood, for they have
Killed God's only Son.

The fear which grasp the soul of man,
For He reached out, to save their souls,
And they cried out, forever no!

GERALD A. GOTT
14 August 1995

FOOT OF THE HILL

Through the narrow streets, of pain
And grief, He carries upon His back,
The teak tree.

A tree of death, sorrows, and tears,
I see Him, as He passes near. The
Crowd cries out, with vengeance, and
Hate, today you die, beyond the gate.

Upon His head, a crown of thorns, which
Pierce His head, blood streams down, upon
The ground, for there is no help, to be found.

He stumbles and falls, there is a lull,
One is summoned, to take the cross, which has
Fallen, against the walls.

Out of the gate, until the foot of the hill, upon
Its sight, there is a chill, the chill of death, which
Stands and waits, just beyond, those broken gates.

A hill known for its pain and grief, the sorrows of
Death, and misery, a hill called Cal'va-ry. Upon the
Tree, they nailed His hands, into the sky, He searched
The winds, His cry went out, ending there, and all below
Could only stare.

He gave His life, upon a tree, on top of a hill, for all to see,
A hill despised, called Cal'va-ry.

GERALD A. GOTT
20 August 1995

9

THE GARDEN

In solitude he kneels and prays,
For all who came with him, that
Faithful day, wait just beyond
A stone's cast away.

Too tired to go and kneel with him, as
He prayed, he saw the end. Drops of sweat,
As if it were blood, fell from his brow, upon the
Dry, and thirsty ground.

Those who came, did not awake, and yet he
Continued on to pray, for all the fear within
His flesh, he knew and felt, and held his breath.

This cup my Father, I beg of thee, please let it pass
Away from me, if be thy will, I shall partake, and know
Thy will, be done this day. Upon the ground, he laid
Out prone, because his Father, was on the throne.

The Father heard, an angel appeared, to comfort and
Strengthen, his only Beloved. For this was the day,
That evil would reign, the Son of God, would truly be
Shamed.

To the cross, he carried the pain, nailed upon the tree
Of death, for all to view, in disbelief, for God himself,
Was on that tree.

GERALD A. GOTT
19 September 1995

ABBA FATHER

I want to cry aloud, My God, why hast
Thou died, for such a wretch like me?
Why did you, take all the spite of man,
With you on the cross?

The suffering and pain, which you endured,
Before the cross, was it so, that I might see,
The love you had, for soul's like me?

Pain which pierced, your very soul. Upon the cross,
When you were nailed. My heart cries out, thy love
For me, I cannot keep.

Abba Father, I fail thee every day, and yet I know,
Thou will always be, a breath away, for thou hast
Always heard my cry, and I felt you, by my side.

My heart ache's, for the love I see, and yet within, this
Darken frame, I only hurt and feel the shame. The shame
Of man, for which I am.

Those which killed thee, years ago, live today for this I know,
For I am one, before the dawn, whose hands upon the cross
Was strong.

Until the day, I saw thy love, my heart astray, not knowing thee,
And yet my Father, you suffered me. Into the heavens, my cry went
Out, in an instant, you had my hand. My heart's anew, with love
For thee, because your love, was shown to me.

Upon a hill, a silent man, nailed upon a lonely tree, for all to
Gaze, and wonder why, my loving Father, freely died.

GERALD A. GOTT
4 October 1995

11

BEFORE THEE

I come before thee, in trembling and fear,
In solitude and silence, my presence appears.
I fear to look upon thee, knowing that I"m
Unworthy, for thy love for me, I cannot understand.

I fear to look upon thy glory, which unfolds
About the heavens, and rejoice in my heart,
For the grace, thou has given.

With fear and joy, I look into your eyes, and
Know within my heart, that thou art truly Christ.
As I bow before my King, I praise the heavens, that
Thou has always reigned.

Unworthy as I am, I know your love, has always been,
For all your creations, especially man. For only man, has
A soul, which shall depart, upon his death, into the heavens,
Or into the depths.

GERALD A. GOTT
4 October 1995

WITHIN

Within this soul, a solemn role, plays
Again each day of light, to find this soul,
Alone at night. Each day and night, this
Soul craves flight, alone from birth, until
Tonight.

Searching heaven for all seems lost, alone
This soul, cries in the dark. All around, are
Like the wind, for this soul, alone is sin

The melodies, which reach the heart, are not
Silent, nor far apart, for this soul, which craves
The light, only finds the hate inside.

Alone at night, for no one cares, this soul alone,
Will surely bear, the emptiness of years gone by,
This soul cries out, my God, why is it I?

GERALD A. GOTT
18 November 1995

HOLY

My mind cannot imagine thy glory, nor
Can I understand thy mercy, thou hast
Shown me, a sinner
Within the sea.

Thy creations are more beautiful, than the eyes
Can comprehend, and yet, without them, the eyes
In darkness, cannot see the love, that is found
Within.

The glory of thy realm, for all to behold, is but
Before us, and yet we turn away, for in the heart
On man, the void is ever present, ever empty, until
That faithful day.

Does the darkness hide thee, like the desert sands?
For all the saints, have seen thee, thy spirit dwells,
Within the heart of man.

Ever present, ever knowing, always loving, always
Caring, never more to hide from me, for I worship
Only thee.

For my God, thou art Holy, in the eyes of all the
World, for my Lord, and King of Kings, your the
One, I want to see.

GERALD A. GOTT
14 January 1996

OPEN WOUNDS

Open wounds to the world this day,
Unto the Father, the Son did pray, for
The souls of those below, for they heard
Not, the words He spoke.

Unto the skies, His eyes did gaze, for the
Sun, was gone that day. Open wounds unto
The heaven's, where God himself, saw only
Love, for His Son, was like the dove.

As the hate, reign high that day, for God himself,
Would surely pay, for the love, He did not hide, for
All the hate, was in mankind.

Unto the heaven's, the cry went out, the Son of God,
Has died this day, for all mankind, will surely pay. But
The love, of God for man, saved the souls, as God had planned.

Open wounds, as blood poured out, dropped upon the open
Ground, the life of Christ, slipped for away, into the silent, end
Of day.

The heaven's cried, and mourned their loss, for only God, knew
Man had lost. But for His love, which He did give, the only hope,
For man's own sin.

GERALD A. GOTT
13 February 1996

IN HIS HANDS

In his hands, He holds me fast, my
Soul alone is saved at last, to find my
Lord, his love abounds, for at last, my
Soul is found.

Adrift like waves, up the sea, the currents
Carry, far beneath, to certain death, for souls
Like me.

In crimson red, I see the dead, no place to heal,
Their broken hearts, for all their souls, shall now
Depart. Unto the depths, of no regain, for only
Death, has brought them pain.

In the hands, of One above, my souls is safe, from
Fire and pain. I bow unto, my Lord above, for He
Alone, has shown His love.

I cry aloud, my Lord and King, I worship thee, for
This I sing, blessed be, the King of Kings. For thou
Has saved, this soul of sand, with thy loving, gentle
Hands.

GERALD A. GOTT
20 February 1996

KING OF KINGS

How majestic is your Name, how the
World, in latter times, have proclaimed,
The beauty of your Word, for all the world,
By now has heard.

The love you showed, upon the hill, as God above the
Darken skies, looked down and heard, your painful cries.
Men in past, as they are now, turn as if, they hear no sound.

Thy Spirit, unto the mortal flesh if man, fulfills the
Empty void, which for ages, is timeless, as it stands.

The welcome cry, of joy from within, clouds the minds,
Of those who call, upon your Name, thy Spirit enters, the
Lonely soul, and takes away the shame.

How sad O' man, that thou hast, denied the living God,
Which cried unto the Father, "Forgive them for they know
Not what they do", for man hast played, the perfect fool.

The wisdom of man, leads to death, the cry unto the
Living God, leads a weary soul, to rest.

GERALD A. GOTT
6 May 1996

WITHOUT THEE

Without thee O'Lord, my God, and my
Strength, there is nothing but anguish
And despair.

I pray my Lord, you leave me not, that thou
Shalt be with me all my days. For without
Thee, there is nothing, no joy, no laughter,
Only pain and sorrow follows my steps.

Embrace me and let me not fall away from thee,
This I make, as my plea. As my life slips away
Day by day, I cling unto thy Word, which states that
I belong to thee.

Without thee O'Lord, my God, my life itself is void,
And lonely. My soul thou hast created and filled with
Thy Spriit, my joy is fulfilled, until thou has called me
Home.

GERALD A. GOTT
30 June 1996

THE LAMB

Upon the hill, there hangs a man, upon a
Cross, which no man sought, but He alone,
Was taken there, for all the world, to see and
Share.

Without the blemish, of man himself, this one
Called, by God alone, as the angels, with bodies
Prone, lay before their Father's throne.

Through the midst of heaven's gate, the sound
Was heard, as if by faith, the Father saw, through
Clouds of furl, his dying Son, and felt the sorrow.

Forgive them, for they know not, what they do,
Cried the lonely figure, hanging in constant
Pain, upon the cross, of wood and shame.

Upon the cross, was God's own Son, for this alone, the
Victory's won. As the lamb receives his throne, all about
Lie still, and prone.

The Lamb looks down, with loving eyes, for all His glory,
Fills heaven's skies.

GERALD A. GOTT
11 July 1996

INTO THY HANDS

Into thy hands, my soul now
Lies, to wonder why, the shell
Has died. Upon departure, one
Hears the cry.

Into the heaven's, where God abides,
For God alone, with searching eyes,
Has saved this soul, from a hellish
Plight.

For thy love, my soul now cleaves,
Inherent peace, shall never leave, thy
Hands alone, are all I need.

Hands once pierced, with spikes of iron, now
Open up, amidst the shroud, to claim the soul,
From wandering crowds.

Into thy hands, my soul now stands, within the
Glory, of thy realm, my comprehension overwhelmed.
Thy beauty, about me, is like the sea.

GERALD A. GOTT
4 February 1997

DISTURBED

Dear Lord, I looked this morning in the mirror
Of your Word, and saw there are reflections, which
Left me disturbed.

Instead the reflections of Christ's own life in me,
I saw the world's own visions, and inconsistencies. I
Took one step closer, and there my eyes could see, the
Image of my Saviour, was lured by my beliefs.

I couldn't see the glory of Jesus, in my face, but my own
Self indulgence in every human way.

Then those quiet moments, between my Lord and I, I realized
A painful emptiness inside. When I reflect the image of myself
In earthly pride, not the love of Jesus, there's a struggle deep inside.

It's when we put the Saviour first, in all we do, the joy of salvation,
To others will show through. Please purify my heart Lord, in moments
Spent with thee, that others who see me, will see thy image, Lord in me.

KRISTINE GOTT
(Gerald's daughter, date unknown)

ETERNAL BLOOD

Eternal Blood, from wounds endured, in
Spite of man, shall never move. Will always bear,
The pain of grief, for man alone, shall reap defeat.

Upon the surface, of wood and shame,
Drips God's blood, with all the pain.
For this day, shall ever stand, in the mind,
And hearts of man.

Tortured soul among the trees, for His love,
Shall always be, even death, which hinders
Man, has no hold, upon the Lamb.

Blood drops run, their lonely course, down the
Cross, of harden souls. The Lamb, with open eyes,
Seeks the Father, in the skies.

In to thy hands, I give my soul, for all around, who stood
Below, heard the cry, from painful lips, the Lamb is
Silent, because of death.

Upon the cross, forever Stained, dripped the blood, from
God's own hands, which stand impaled, in time, for man.

GERALD A. GOTT
29 April 1997

FATHER IS IT TIME?

With weary eyes, of unrest, which
Stare astray, and fail the test, slightly
With a gleam of hope, rest the eyes,
Which no one knows.

Pain within, for no one sees, are eyes
Of hope and searching glee. For darkness
Shrouds, the rays of hope, while looking
On, this lonely soul.

Time has passed, this empty void, for if
You listen, you hear the Voice. Empty eyes,
That stare amist, seeking substance, where
Pain exists.

Fears consumes, the very soul, numbs the mind,
As crystals blow. Father, is it time? For this
Question, is on my mind. Only depths, of time
Itself, will clear the air, of shame and guilt.

For the glimmer, in the eyes, seem to fade, as distant lights.
Only pain, of death itself, shall relieve this soul, which knelt,
Before the Lord, of ancient days, this soul alone, shall kneel
And pray.

GERALD A. GOTT
7 May 1997

THE CUP

Within the cup, lay no man's hand, but
Memories of, the Son of Man. The Son
Of Man, shall drink again, when time itself,
Fulfills the deed, which God alone, shall
Surely see.

For the blood, which fell that day, purged the
Sins, of man away. Yet within, the pride of
Man, stands the door, of self proclaim. Who
Is Christ? That we should bow, for we are men,
And very proud.

The cup again, shall be lifted up, for all mankind,
Shall surely see, the heavens open, in glorious splendor,
For God Himself, shall not be hindered.

For the love, has gone astray, away from man, that solemn day.
Upon the hills, of death and shame, for the sin, of man remains.
Forever in, the world of time, for God Himself, gave up His life.

GERALD A. GOTT
19 August 1997

LONELY HOUR

Lonely hour, for death to kill, for
God's own Son, on Gol'go-tha's hill,
To look upon, the empty land, for the
Souls, took not His hand.

Upon the ground, they sat and watched, for
Death to come, which blood had bought. Mocking
Him, as death approached, taking all and making note.

Those beside Him, cast their eyes, upon the One, beneath
The skies, in painful breaths, they cried in fear, for only
Death, was standing near.

Darkness filled, the very skies, which felt the pain, and
Heard their cries. The Son, cried out, why hast though forsaken
Me? A lonely death, upon the tree.

Below the cross, of death and pain, for in the darkness, was
Only shame. For man again, in foolish pride, killed the One,
Whose love abides.

GERALD A. GOTT
29 July 1997

THE CROSS

The tree is grown, the timber used,
Save one piece, for man's own tool.

The tool of death, awaits one man,
It's lonely course, drifts to its end.
No stain appears, nor chips defray,
The beauty of, this tool of prey.

As the tree, is carved at last,
Into the cross, which holds him fast,
For the stakes, which pierced his flesh,
Has pierced the tool, which comes to rest,
Upon the hill, of no return,
For the cross, shall not be burned.

For the blood, which drips and stains,
The tree no longer, shall remain,
Upon the hill, of death and pain.
For the victim, at last is free,
His lifeless body, from the tree.

All are gone, as silence waits, the tree now stained,
And bruised within, its beauty gone, its shame begins,
For all the world, shall always see, the tool of death, was that one tree.

GERALD A. GOTT
5 January 1998

HUMBLE SOUL

Tears which fell, upon the skin, to wash away,
The dirt of sin, unto the body, of One so righteous,
The tears of one, who's soul, now broken.

Wipes away the tears of dread, with the hairs, upon
Her head, knowing now with sadden heart, the One
She cleans, shall soon depart.

Ointment upon thy feet, with love applied, within my soul,
My hearth doth cry. The Master's feet, for which I gaze, I
Touch for now, with reverent fear, for my love, He knows
Is near.

Upon His feet, my lips now meet, with humble heart, and
Broken soul, I bow my spirit, for He shall know, the darken
Path, which I have followed, has led me to, the One who sees,
The trail of sin, which follows me.

With mercy in His eyes, He speaks to me, for I have seen, your
Love for Me. He speaks again, to only me, "thy faith has saved
Thee, go in peace."

GERALD A. GOTT
22 January 1998

SILENTLY THEY WATCHED

Silently they watched, as the King, struggled
To the hill, the hill of death. Soldiers amazed, because of the
Silent form, which slowly made His way,
To the hill, of no return.

Eyes widen beyond belief, for this One, found no
Relief, as spikes tore, through flesh and bone, the cries of
Those, of sorrow heard.

As the cross, was dropped, within the ground, a thud was heard,
With a chilling sound, for the One, upon the tree, whose life was
Shed, would soon greet death.

Soldiers gambled, for His clothes, as death came nearer, ever so
Close, but not to touch, those below. For death had come, to claim
The man, for God Himself, in grieving pain, had died for all, which
Sin had claimed.

Eyes upon heaven's door, the sound came forth, from broken
Lips, which spoke no more, unto thy hands, my soul I give, for thou art
King,
My Father dear.

The heaven's wept, the earth did shake, all around the people strove, within
The wake. Fear swept through, as shock absorbed, the numbing minds,
which
Now have killed, the only One, which came to save, a darken world, of
lonely
Souls, immersed in sin.

GERALD A. GOTT
25 December 2002

WHERE ARE THOU

I know that many years ago, I found you
Within my soul. For I called for thee, within
An instant, I was free.

The joy I felt, because the weight was gone,
Untold blessing fell upon my life, so near you
Were, every darken night.

My walk with thee, was strangely nimble and very weak,
For I had to learn, to walk with thee. Never knowing
Where you would lead.

As I grew, within your word, I learned to preach, from
What I heard, and yet your word was true to form, never
Changing from the norm.

As the years, have now gone by, I find that I, at times am
Blind. For I see, your word is true, and yet I wonder, where
Am I?

I know that, within my heart, you never left me, nor closed
Your ears, to hear my cries, for I am weak, and sometimes
Blind.

I read your word, in early day, I often wonder, what I should pray,
I want to serve thee, with all my heart, and yet I wonder, what
Is my part.

Loving Father, hear my cry, for I am old now, and wonder why, you
Never left me, but I did you, I only wish our love would bloom.

GERALD A. GOTT
11 November 2006

FOOTPRINTS

As the solemn weary crowd, gathers
Far beneath the clouds, of heaven's gate
Now open wide. Stand the angels before the
Throne, and sing their praise, for another
Soul.

But the crowd cannot hear, the sounds of joy
Above the clouds, for in sorrow, tears abound
As the bearers, come down the hill. For they carry
Within their grasp, a soul now gone, which no one
Knows, stands above the lonely clouds.

Looking down above the crowd, praising God for
He alone, saved this soul, from eternal darkness far below.
Now as the angels, gather him with joy delight, he now waits
For some below. For in the future, they as he, shall stand
Together, before the King.

GERALD A. GOTT
10 October 2011

FORSAKEN

Alone upon the tree, hung the man who died for me,
With darken skies shutting out the sun, no more
Shall the brightness gleam, in the darkness of
Rebuke.

Man again has forced his way, into the hearts,
Which have been swayed, to kill the One, in purity,
Taking light from the world, keeping darkness
With its peril.

But in death, came life, never ending, forever
With us, defeating death, fear, and pain. For His
Death, was our gain.

Upon the tree, with darken skies, the death
Of man, before our eyes, never knowing the
Reason why.

Until the day, He rose again, defeating death
And giving life, for those believers will rise
Again. Singing praises to His name, before the
Throne, of King of Kings.

GERALD A. GOTT
14 November 2013

ON BENDED KNEE

On bended knee, with head bowed down,
I dare not look up, before the crown. For
I know upon the throne, sits the one, who
Died alone.

Pain which tore his soul apart, for so many
Turned their hearts, for the light which, shined
So bright, showed his love, but man was blind.

Every knee bowed down, for all the souls which
Gather round, in silence they wait, some knowing
Not, if they themselves, shall see the King, for which
They wait, on bended knees.

Other souls giving praise, for they know this
Very day, the Savior sits upon the throne, the
Sound of thunder, in His voice, for all the souls,
Who had a choice.

Joy and fear filled the air, for all were listening,
Their soul's now bare, before the throne, for
All to share.

I must go, my name now called, to see my King
Upon the throne. I love my Savior, and hear His
Voice, I lift my head, wipe tears aside, for all the
Wonders, before my eyes.

GERALD A. GOTT
30 December 2013

SHADOW OF THE CROSS

In the shadow of the cross,
Lies the darkness, within man's
Heart, where light might shine, and
Given sight, now hidden within, the
Shadow's plight.

A lone figure, held captive, in pain
And agony, for man again, has shown
His depravity.

In the shadow of the cross, where darkness
Did abound, lie the soul's, which now have
Passed, they cry a forbidden sound.

Now the skies, turn dark and violent, as
The figure's, voice is silent, giving up the
Life, he had, for the soul's, upon the land.

The cross now empty, alone between the two,
The shadow mixed, between the sun and moon,
A symbol of love, for me and you.

GERALD A. GOTT
1 June 2014

TEARS BEFORE THE THRONE

As I humbly, kneel beneath, the
Throne before me, I cry within,
My soul still broken, for the sins,
Which now are spoken.

For my sins, like waves upon the sea,
Breaking before me, on bended knees.
The voice I hear, sounds like thunder,
With searching eyes, I seek his face, for
In my heart, I won the race.

For the sins, before the throne, have
Been covered, and are no more, for in
The Light, which shines above, has
Covered them, with his own blood.

The darkness which, I once beheld, no
Longer with me, now lies in hell, for the
Light, above the heaven's, has called my
Name, my spirit soar's, above the clouds,
No longer held, by doubting crowds.

GERALD A. GOTT
16 November 2014

CALVARY'S TEARS

Beneath the cross, are
Questioning eyes, seeking
Answers and wondering why.

As grieving souls, look upon the
Man, whose lifeless body, broken
By blows, hangs in despair, for all
Those below.

Forever in time, in silent despair, the
Heaven's of glory, shall always declare,
The blood of the lamb, forever will stand.
Mindless men, with blood on their hands.

Echo's of sorrow's, are heard on the hill,
Heart's which are crumbled, in pieces they
Fall, in silence and darkness, they cry to
Us all.

For in time, all men will have known, the
Cross, in the center, shall all way's, be
Told, fasten so tightly, our savior was held,
For man's own vengeance, has brought his
Own hell.

GERALD A. GOTT
4 January 2015

Heaven

ANGELS

Upon the heavens the angels fly, upon
The earth, they cast their eye, only man who
Cannot see, the angel's plight, upon the seas.

The wing's unfold, as flowers bloom, as the
Angels appear like dew, for only man, and man
Alone, can't see the angels, who left their home.

Around us all, each day and night, the angels
Pass, in endless flight, man can't see, nor hear
Their cry.

Only God, who sent them here, knows the reason,
Why angels hear, His voice alone, from heaven's
Gate, for the angels, passed this way.

Into the skies, from which they came, the angels
Fly, away in shame, for in their quest, man cursed
His name, for only man, can be so vain.

Into the heaven's, the angels fly, as the Master
Hears their cries, we've completed the task at hand,
For all the hope, is gone from man.

As the heaven's gates are closed, and the Master's
Hands unfold, the angels' cry, into the Light, our
Lord and King, shall they all die?

GERALD A. GOTT
1 November 1995

37

HEAVEN'S CRYING

Feel the winds, as they cascade by,
Often blowing blossom's, from their
Cradle, into the darken skies.

Hear the thunder, as it reaches down,
Blaring loud about you, nowhere to be found.
See the crystals falling, eyes upon the clouds,
As the moisture softens, endless fields, around.

Grief in broken pieces, falling all about, no one knowing,
Why the heaven's shout, sorrow is now falling, upon the
Open ground.

Heaven is now crying, tear drops can't return, for the
Clouds of thunder, cover most the earth. Only sheets of
Lightning, seen by crystal's light, know the lonely reason,
Tear drops, fell tonight.

GERALD A. GOTT
20 February 1997

LITTLE ANGEL

Little hands which never grasp, thy
Mother's hand, nor feet that touched,
Thy father's brow, nor eyes so bright,
With life's delight, our soul's which
Grieve, throughout the night.

For God has taken, with love and care,
The cherished one, we loved so dear. Our
Cries are heard, with much despair, darken
Days which now abode, for we are left, alone
And cold.

Death has come, and left a void, but life has
Come, with a still voice, peace my children,
For I have need, of thy child, beside my knee.

Dry thy tears, within thy soul, for she is with me,
Looking up, with gleeful eyes, no pain nor sorrow,
Shall ever fall, upon my angel, for whom I called.

Find solace children, within thy soul's, for thy child,
Which thou hast known, amongst the thousands, of
Little souls, which surround, my very Throne.

GERALD A. GOTT
14 October 2002

TEAR DROPS FROM ABOVE

Feel the tears, from above, for darkness
Falls, upon the skies. Caring not, where
Souls do hide. One would ask, the reason
Why, for all the clouds, appear to cry.

Looking up, from far beneath, seeking answers
I cannot keep, as the rain drops, fall upon my
Brow, for the answers, I have not found.

Why the tears, from heaven's face, fall upon
The human race, giving life, when death appears,
Knowing not, why all the tears.

My brow now wet, from all the rain, I hurry on,
In hope of gain, for poorer days, I left behind, to
Seek my fortune, within the skies.

In seeking fortune, which was my goal, I left behind
Which once was told, love is stronger, than any wealth,
For in the end, thy soul shall melt.

GERALD A. GOTT
3 January 2014

40

WITHIN THE CLOUDS

Transparent to the eyes
Below, ever searching, for
This I know, wonders from the
Distant gates, just beyond, our
Blinded gaze.

Deep within the hidden blue, forms
Which search, outside the hue, seeking
Substance of no return, for in the heat,
They all but burned.

Eyes below, searching depths, in the
Distance, beyond man's reach, is the
Glory, and blessed peace. Eternal time
Shall never pass, for we have reached,
Our home at last.

GERALD A. GOTT
19 March 2015

Love

SANDY

The widow's arms, that do unfold
Upon my body for which they hold.
I seek thy mercy for what it is,
I seek thee dear, for just one kiss.

The kiss that will go on forever,
And thy love shall never perish,
For deep inside, my inner thoughts,
My mind, itself, shall never want,
The love of, but a few, and yet my dear,
It shall be you.

I loathe the fear of lonely depths,
And yet my dear, I have not slepth.
My bed is empty and still within,
For you have gone on journey's end.

Thy life has ended, thy shall not wake.

For in the sleep of no return,
My love for thee shall always burn.

GERALD A. GOTT
Unknown Date
~ 1994

COMFORTING HANDS

The days are gone,
When she was young,
So naïve, and yet
So strong.

The years have passed,
Her beauty faded, like
The clouds of day, which
Seem to linger, then disappear.

Her children no longer young,
And spry, have grown, with
Families of their own.

She was always busy working
Day and night, she had no time,
To see her plight

Their noise, which engulfed
Their home, is no more, they're
All gone, she's all alone.

Alone she sits, thinking of times
Which were in the past, only to
Realize, time has passed

Alone she sits, each day and night,
For now she has the time, to see
Her plight, which is ever before her
Throughout the night.

There are times, when loneliness,
Engulfs her very soul, but she,
And I know, she's not alone.

She can't feel, the gentle hands,
Which surrounds her, with loving care.
The voice which says, I am here, fear not,
Be not afraid, I am with you, all the day.

As the sun sets, within her sight, a
Sigh of fear, escapes her breath, only
She knows, it is not death.

The voice, which only she can
Hear, calls and reassures, this
Fragile soul, all is well, I am
Here, you're not alone.

She still trembles, and is afraid,
Of lonely nights, which come her way.
Within her soul, she knows, she's not alone.

She knows Him, whose name is above
All names, who gave His life, that
She might have life.

Her eyelids close, with a smile
Upon her face, for she knows, because
Of Him, she can face another day.

GERALD A. GOTT
16 January 1995

45

KRISTINE

Little dumpling of my eye, how
I love thee, from deep inside.
Close they little eye lids now,
That they might sleep, please
Lie down.

I see you peeping from covers fold,
My little dumpling, you hands are cold.
I see that smile, which glows like the
Brightness of the sun, I know my
Dumpling, you're having fun.

Little dumpling of my life, please
Close they lids upon your eyes. Sleep
My dumpling, please sleep tonight, in
The morning, when you awake, we'll go
Outside and play all day.

At end of day, there comes a time,
Please my dumpling, please sleep tonight.

GERALD A. GOTT
Re-written 14 April 1995

DEAREST ONE

How I worried my little one,
Your life's so small, it's just begun.
For the fear I feel for you, and
Know one day, you'll leave me soon.

Like a flower, that's grown so tall,
To reach the sun, and find it all,
One day soon, you won't be small, and
You will seek, another call.

How I love you with all my heart, and
Know one day, you will depart, for all
The love I have for you, embraces like
The morning dew.

You cannot see, nor understand, the
Pain I feel, when death's at hand. In
The world of no return, you nor I, shall
Ever see, the joy and love, you gave to me.

For today, is only now, so let us smile,
Forget the frown, for tomorrow yet another
Day, for you and I, to love and play.

GERALD A. GOTT
2 June 1995

THY LOVE IS MINE

In time gone by, when you were young, the
Days have come, and nights have passed,
My love for thee, shall ever last.

In years one sees, the strength of time,
Through many heartache's, I found you mine,
For God alone, has given thee, thy hand in
Marriage, to only me.

My soul shall always bear,
My love for thee, I
Shall not share

Upon my death, weep not for me, for God
Alone has given thee, your love, my dear,
To only me.

GERALD A. GOTT
20 August 1995

LONELY HEARTS

From the sadness far within, I often wonder
How it begin, often times there were disputes, but
In their hearts, laid solid roots.

Until one day, the roots did stray, for in the
Soil, of decay, the strength was gone, no more
To show, for without the root, no love could grow.

Then the love, had turn to hate, for each heart
Denied the day, which came about, in darken clouds,
For the hearts, went underground.

No more to love, and seek the day, for all the love,
Had passed away. Lonely times ahead you see, for
My love, was for thee.

GERALD A. GOTT
3 January 1996

MY LOVE

To watch and seek, and never ask, my
Soul within me, cries out in stillness,
Never close, and yet not far.

To say the things, I cannot speak,
My words are few, and
Often weak. Fears within my very heart, is
Like the void, I cannot touch.

To grasp the air, I cannot hold, is like
The sand, in windless nights, so still and
Solemn, and always free, and yet my heart,
Cries out to thee.

You are blinded, and cannot see, nor can
You hear, my empty pleas. When at dusk, the
Sun seems near, to touch and feel, without the
Fear.

T's death I seek, to end this state, to find myself,
And never wake. Within the darkness, of fear itself,
I find the void, inside my soul, the heartless world, I've
Always known.

GERALD A. GOTT
14 January 1996

ONCE AGAIN

To touch your hand, once again, to
See your smile, and feel the warmth,
For those are times, for now are gone.

To feel the hurt, within your heart, as
Tear drops crash, upon the ground. To
Feel the softness of your hair and know
That you, often cared.

To see your walk, in someone else, makes
Me smile, and sometimes melt, to know that
You're no longer here, brings me grief, with
Much despair.

To touch your hand, just once again, would
Lift my heart, where you began.

GERALD A. GOTT
28 January 1996

TEARS IN THE RAIN

As the drops fall from the sky, I
Often think, and wonder why, my
Love for thee, has always been, I
Thank the Lord, that you were sent.

Thunder roars from heaven's fold, as
The tear drops, in silence cold, seem to
Start, from one's own soul.

My love for thee, is like the wind, always
There, free to win. Coldness shrouds my
Inner heart, for I know not, where thou art.

As the tears fall, with the rain, my heart is
Broken, from all the pain, for in the skies, I
See the light, and know full well, my lonely plight.

To touch your hand, to feel your pulse, to know that
You, and I shall touch, brings the rivers, of untold wealth,
For your love, I surely felt.

I move away, as depths of clay, to stand and watch, the skies
Turn gray, for my tears, just as the rain, shall fall again, upon
Your grave.

GERALD A. GOTT
2 April 1996

SILENT LOVE

In silent years, now gone by, the
Only love, is in their cry, for in the
Wind, a voice drifts by, for all the
Love, is gone tonight.

So many years, which had been here, are
No longer found, amongst the tears, for
Time itself, has passed away, just as the
Tears, alone do fade.

The empty heart, a void of solitude,
Rest within the empty, darken room. For
No warmth is found, only coldness, as
Broken limbs, upon the ground.

Silence is the enemy, which no one seems
To find, for within the lonely void, the enemy
Seems to hide.

Silent love, which no one hears, is ever present,
Through the years, always present, always near,
For in this love, there is no fear.

GERALD A. GOTT
10 August 1996

MY LOVE

I see and yet I cannot touch, for
Thy soul is weak, within my very
Being, the walls cry out and weep.

To see you once again, strong and
Vibrant, to hear your voice, as yesterday,
For this I surely pray.

Within thy body, lifeless as it seems, you
Breath, is but a whisper, your pulse is faint, as
The moon rising, above the crest, your body
Still, as if in final rest.

My mind wanders, seeking ways to help, and
Yet I know within, thy life escapes, from the
Very hands, for which they hold.

Doom of darkness, appears before my eyes, for
All the hope, has fled, into the darken night.
Through the shadows, hands appear before thy soul,
Reaching in to take, the life to shores unknown.

Fear abounds within my soul, for thy life, I want
To hold, and keep it, from the shores, of darken tides,
And lonesome coves.

GERALD A. GOTT
21 November 1996

LOST MOMENTS

There were days, when we could talk,
And never know, when it was dark.
There were days, when we could laugh,
To watch the children, as they played.
There were days, when love was new,
Perfect innocence, beneath the moon,
There were days, with children near,
We together, knew no fear.
There were days, when tears which fell,
Came to rest, upon the sill.
Now the days, seem far away,
For the children, no longer play.
All the laughter, no longer heard,
For the souls, have fled like birds.
Alone and quiet, the two of us, wandering when, we left the rush.
Quietly knowing, within our hearts,
Our time together, will soon depart.
To catch the time, and whispers lost,
For in our hearts, we want them caught.
Never more, to leave again, to hold them captive, when time began.

GERALD A. GOTT
Unknown Date
~2001

TOUCH ME NOT

Touch me not, my dear at all, for the
Time, has come at last. Now I leave, with
Heavy heart, and weaken bones, for only
Strength, is in my soul.

Days gone by, to touch again, only sadness
Waves goodbye, for my love, for thee alone,
In brightness shines, for the years, have been
So kind.

Fret not for the soul, now gone, for you alone,
Shall always know, where this soul, shall always be.
For the King, has called my name, in haste, I leave
To see the King.

Upon the clouds, my soul now rests, before the King,
With loving arms, He guides to eternal rest, no more
Tears, nor grieving heart, for you my dear, shall
Never part.

GERALD A. GOTT
11 April 2005

LONELY MIST

Surrounded by the ever mist, of morning dew,
Always leads me, my dear to you. For our love,
Forever be, shared with no one, but only me.

Early dew drops, from above, reminds me of,
Our eternal love, always there, but not in sight,
For I grieve, throughout the night.

O' to touch, thee once again, for our love, shall
Always stand, as trees of strength, never wavering,
Within the wind, silent as the ever breeze, always
There, never seen.

I shall see, thee once again, in the Kingdom, which
Awaits, for the Lord, has told us so, where I am, you
Shall go. Soon my dear, we will meet, within the
Clouds, of our King.

GERALD A. GOTT
1 March 2007

FADED MEMORIES

To know the reason why, my love has
Left and died. All the laughter, joy and
Fun, now faded beneath the sun.

Holding hands in day light joy, for did
I know, the hidden ploy. When darkness
Came, that faithful day, I sat in loneliness,
And began to pray.

Alone again, after many years, what am
I to do, as I sat with broken heart, knowing
This would happen, from the start.

Silent rooms await my presence, with no
Laughter, for all is empty, beneath the
Rafters. How I miss my love today, forever
Gone, I shall not sway, until my death, my
Love for thee, shall always last, until we meet.

GERALD A. GOTT
9 January 2014

FORGOTTEN TIMES

There were days when love was new,
Fresh as new day snow, for all to know,
Caring not about the world's cares, for
Love was in the air.

Centered on thy love before thee, knowing
Not the days ahead, for in the future, was
Not at hand, for only now, our love did stand.

Through the years, as time did pass, did we now
Know, our love did last, beyond our dreams, of
Yesterday, our souls together, seek for another
Way.

Years have taken, a heavy toll, upon the two,
O' broken souls, as love now dwindled, so far away,
Seeking yet, another day.

In the arms, of death so soon, they have each
Other, beneath the moon. Now their love, entwine
Forever, shall evermore be together.

GERALD A. GOTT
22 February 2014

HEART STRINGS

The weaken state, of heart's content, has left
Aside, the void within, no longer light, for deep
Inside. With fear of pain, lies the clouds, without
The rain.

Searching why, thy love is gone, knowing not the
Reason why, the darken clouds, now fill the sky.
Alone again, without the smile, for now my heart,
Must rest a while.

Longing for, the crimson ties, which once had, our
Hearts abide, for the shore, of shallow waters,
Keep the life, of souls now hollow.

Within the crystals, seeing in, lies the hearts,
Held within, caring not for life itself, for their
Heart's now torn apart. Lies in pieces evermore,
Washing on the distant shores.

GERALD A. GOTT
21 March 2014

BROTHERS

When we were young, always seeking
Way's to have fun, ever running, searching,
For new adventurers, knowing not, what
Harm lay ahead.

Together we stood, alone and afraid, forever
With fear, was to meet us, this day. Shouting
And cursing, never away, all we wanted to do,
Is continue to play.

Where was the warmth, of love never told, o'
To hear, with kindness and strength, the word's
Never spoken, because hell was intrenched.

Even today, in some way alone, thanking the
Lord, for mercy was shone. Heartbreaks ahead,
And now in the past, thinking of love one's, and
Feeling so sad.

GERALD A. GOTT
13 January 2015

LOVE UPON THE ROCKS

O' thy love, for which I had, never
Ending, never sad, upon the water's
Of shining glass.

The warmth within my soul, to keep,
Never worried, for love is deep. Tender
Yearnings for you alone, upon the rocks,
Thy love below.

All the lies and deceit, lie before my
Trembling feet, my heart now broken,
Within my soul, on to the darken lonely
Shore. In pieces lie the love for thee, as
Morning break's, no one to see.

The tears which fall, upon the rocks,
Will wash away, as sunset falls, never
To, return to me, for my love, washed
Out to sea.

GERALD A. GOTT
23 August 2015

Loneliness

STILLNESS OF LIFE

In the stillness of no return, I look and
Listen, my eyes search out, the calmness
Of the day, my ears alert, for any play.

How silently the river runs, upon the
Rocks, the waters flow, toward the end, for
No one knows, where the waters, shall ever flow.

The trees so still, and tall in grace, for they
Reach out, into the day. Leaves afresh, with colors
Bright, upon the moon, they glare at night.

Meadows, just beyond the creek, alive with
Life, which I can't see. Within the blades, of
Grass so still, I know there's life, that I can't feel.

Within the skies, so vast and wide, I seek a sign,
Of one small life. In the stillness of the clouds, I
Hear the cry, of sparrows found.

Within the shack, on river's edge, a silent soul, sits
On the bed, looking up into the skies, asking, wondering,
Why might I, be the one, in silent streams, for all my
Visions, are only dreams.

GERALD A. GOTT
22 January 1996

SEARCHING

I awake and wonder where, you alone are
Yet not near, for I tremble, with new found fear,
Alone again within my sphere.

I cry aloud within my soul, my eyes search out,
My heart unknown. Where is He, my heart does
Seek, and yet I search, the endless seas. Of those
Who wander, far beneath.

I leave the room, in search of thee, and cast my
Eyes, upon the breeze, perhaps by chance, a glimpse
Of thee, will come about, amongst the trees.

My eyes now glazed, as glass appears, for now
I know, my greatest fear, my love of life, is nowhere
Near.

As crystals fall, upon the ground, my soul has left, and
Can't be found, for love alone, with endless flight, shall
Disappear, into the night.

Crushed as weeds, upon the path, my heart turns cold, as
Ice turns glass, within my silent, painless death.

GERALD A. GOTT
19 March 1996

LEAVING

He stood tall and strong, he seemed
Taller than the mountain tops, the struggle
Was on, with no help to be found.

The furry lasted for what seemed like hours,
Words were said, and blood was spilled, the
Lonely figure, beaten, bruised, and torn, looked
About, with eyes of scorn.

He had taken six of their best, but failed the test, as
Small eyes peered from their hiding place, the figure
Looked down, with sorrow and no place to hide, he
Appeared array, but yet afraid.

There were ten that took him away, that hot and sunny
Day, for he did not return, until the night of the storm, as
He entered, I recognized the form, but now he was moving
Like a beaten dog, slowly, ever so slowly.

As these small eyes looked into the giant's eyes, there was
Sorrow, fear, and defeat. But he will always be strong, stand
Tall, and be unwavering, or so it seemed.

GERALD A. GOTT
18 June 1996

OUTCAST

I stand alone, with time itself, and
Find within, the void of time, for now
It's gone, just like the chime.

Looking up the casting eye, sees nothing
But, the empty sky, for time has passed, when
Skies were full, and now their empty, lifeless
Droll.

All about, and yet alone, for time has come, and
Stood with some, but I'm without, the inner fold,
For time itself, has taken hold, of empty years,
Within my soul.

For this I know, the time has come, for me to leave,
The shining sun, to go and be, with Light itself, my
Broken soul, and tattered will.

GERALD A. GOTT
26 August 1996

ALONE

'Tis life I see, about the wind,
Amongst the trees, as evening
Breaks, I look about, for just one
Mate.

With time alone, stands the soul, which no
One knows, free as darken skies, which peer
Beyond, those searching eyes.

Alone in silence, where time has stopped,
Stands the soul, reaching out, only vapors
Swirl about, the lonely soul, with only doubt.

All about the cries of laughter, are the souls, of
New born clamor, far within the sunken skies,
Are the souls, that have but died.

Here I stand, with soul in hand, seeking others
Where I have been, and yet I see not, the souls
Within, for the soul, alone, still stands.

GERALD A. GOTT
14 November 1996

LONELY DISTANCE

Lonely distance in the wind, for
I find, within the breeze, that I alone,
Am standing free.

Fear not, for the empty nest, alone
Within, the feather's rest. Born to see
The world go by, for in the distance, is
Where they lie.

Touching not, currents which flow, upon
The lonely, broken souls. In the depths, of
No return, shall the void, forever spurn.

To find again, empty shells, looking for, their
Souls in hell. Blacken with the stench of death,
For the souls, in darkness met.

Again the cries, which no one hears, are only lives,
Which now appear, before the souls, which stand in
Fear.

In the distance, is where they met, where it began,
Beyond the depths. Lonely as, the distance long, is
Where you hear, their shattered song.

GERALD A. GOTT
23 April 1998

SILENT CRYSTALS

Hear the voices, of the crystals, falling
As the wind chimes, call. Wonder of
Their beauty, in purity, no longer, held,
Within the depths, of sadden souls, no
Longer kept.

Looking through crystals light, no more pain,
Nor sinless guilt. For death has claimed, the guilt
And pain, as crystals hidden, within the Shawl.

Searching for, a coven dark, where only silence,
Will hear their fall. Only Angels see their pain,
Holding vessels, with crystals light, catching crystals,
In their flight.

Landing softly, in midstream, for the Angles, heard
Their screams. Comfort now, forever more, for the
Crystals, have reached the shore.

Glowing in their haven's rest, crystals fallen become
A light, for the crystals, in darken skies, have a beckon,
To guide their fall, for if you listen, you hear their call.

GERALD A. GOTT
2 June 1998

SHROUD OF LONELINESS

Covered by the depths of night, with
Only fear within my sight's, coming forth
With winter's wind, I find my shroud, is but
Within.

Casting doubt, before my eyes, for all to see,
And wonder why. For time again, has passed
Me by, for all are gone, alone am I, to see the
Shroud, before my eyes.

Succumb by cold, in winter's hold, no more to
Laugh, with sounds of joy, for lonely hours, await
My call, to grasp and hold, of memories lost.

Friends no more, to call my name, to hear the sound,
Of pleasant fame, alone I stand, upon this earth, knowing
Death as if by birth, has come along, to take my soul, upon
That long, and lonely road.

GERALD A. GOTT
28 October 1998

Fear

WALLS WITHOUT MERCY

Within the stillness of this room, the pain
Which roams, like fear and doom, drives
Within the very soul, like harden steel, and
Bitter cold.

The grief is felt, within their hearts, to tear
Apart, the inner self. The stomach churns, the
Pain begins, the spirit prevails, which is of sin.

In the room from silent walls, the crowd stands
Up, and begins to shout, with no reason, nor sanity,
As I wonder, is it me?

Without mercy, the stake is struck, into the heart of
The silent one, until the end of night has come, for all
Have left, and no one won.

Only grief, with much despair, has left the room, which
Is upstairs. For all the fear which was outside, now clings
To us, from deep inside.

For the evening stars appear, upon the crowd, which has
No fear, until the early morning sun, breaks the skies, on
Souls now burned.

GERALD A. GOTT
16 December 1995

GULF

As I peer into the day, the night has
Vanished, and gone away, to reappear
In darkest night, for all have fled, because
Of fright.

Why O man are thee afraid? Yet appears
Another day, for all mankind, shall surely pay.
Within the very depth of man, lies the seed, of
Death within.

The grief is felt, within thy soul, for only God,
Will surely know, the reason why, the death of
Man, shall come at last, and take him home.

For we see, far down the road, as death awaits,
Hands stretched out, so still and cold, to grasp the
Flesh, of man who knows, for surely death, will take
His soul.

Far within the darkest pit, lies the souls, of soundless
Men, for their cries, shall never win, the light of day,
Nor warmth of Son, for their souls, will ever burn.

GERALD A. GOTT
10 January 1996

FOOTSTEPS

In the stillness of the night, the
Sounds of fear, come through the
Walls, for the fear, in in the hall.

To sleep no more, to seek the cause,
To hear the sound, which wakes us all.

The voice of hate, cries out in vain, no
Reply, for no one came. To sleep again,
No soul can do, for the voice, is in the room.

The fear has crept, within us all, to know not
When, we all shall fall, upon the rocks, without
A call.

To reach out, and grab the fear, to rest awhile, without
The hate, for I lost, again today. The fear arises, as
Evening sets in, the sounds of fear, arise again.

To hear those steps, in twilight hours, breaks a
Sweat, upon my brow, for the fear, is present now.
In the night, the steps return, in my mind, forever burned.

GERALD A. GOTT
14 Juanuary 1996

SKELETONS

Fight upon the rock, of death, until
The end, of life and breath. For all
The fear, within their eyes, shows where
Death, shall surely hide.

For in the souls, of mortal men, sleeps the
Fear, of death within, how brave they show,
Their strength indeed, until the sound, of
Death, they meet.

Upon the rock, of death, is life, to grasp and
Hold, until its sides, until the blood, flows
From their wounds, the sound of death, now
Beckons you.

No life within, which holds the sword, for
Life has gone, upon the shores, fight until the
Very end, for only bone, and marrow, mend.

GERALD A. GOTT
22 January 1996

WITHIN THE MIST

Silently vapors engulf the souls of
Men, never to touch, their fears within.

Cries of horror, shall be heard, for in the
Mist, death claims their souls, lost in time,
Their souls alone, forevermore, are free to roam.

Moisture dampens, with a chilling cold, for
All are lost, through searching eyes, for the
Mist, in darken skies.

Erie are the lonely sounds, which aren't heard,
Above the ground, underneath the green array,
Lies the souls, alone, decayed.

For the mist, has engulfed their souls, and
Captured spirit, wills, and bones, for the mist,
Upon the stones, silently waits, in stillness cold.

GERALD A. GOTT
11 December 1996

WOLVES OF PREY

Run as I might, I find that land,
Escapes my flight, into the night.
Sightless eyes search to and fro, for
There is no one, here I know.

Sunken heart, within my frame, for all
The world, to see my shame. Reaching
Out, to touch the void, finding nothing,
Except my voice.

I feel their breath, as fear stands near, I
Know their eyes, search through the night,
To find this soul, alone tonight.

A piercing sound, which holds the breath, of
Every creature, this sound has met. Thistles moving
Along the trail, for the sound, causes hearts to fail.

Into the night, a silent cry, of death itself, without
A sigh. Quickly as, the rushing winds, empty sounds,
Are heard again

GEARLD A. GOTT
28 May 1997

STEPS TO THE UNKNOWN

Steps I hear, with constant
Fear, forever lead to sleepless
Nights, for fear alone, is not in sight.

Alone again, the sweet serenity of
Time now passed, leaves the steps,
I hear to laps.

Cry aloud as I might, the steps I hear,
Within the night, shall bring again, the
Fear and pain, for this night, the steps
Shall gain.

Entry into, my very soul, to feel no warmth,
No embers grow, for fear has taken, my very soul,
My life is ending, forever cold.

The steps which draw, so very near, are from the
One, I count but dear. In the distant, echoes bring,
All the years, of grief and pain.

For in the shallow, frame of man, lies the endless,
Shield of shame, only time, which never ends, brings
Relief, in death for sin.

GERALD A. GOTT
14 July 1997`

EYES

Looking down above the mist, seeing
All without a miss, upon the souls
Upon the sift.

All within the sphere of light, searching
Earth with hidden fears, ever searching
Which stands so near.

Again they look with dead blank eyes,
For what they search for, is deep inside.
Within themselves they cannot find, the
Light of life, which is inside.

So they search throughout the night,
Never knowing their darken plight. Alone
In darkness, seeking light, always searching
In the night.

GERALD A. GOTT
13 October 2013

SHADOW OF TEARS

Within the pain, which no one sees,
Lies the darkness, upon dead seas.
For grief itself, with fear around,
Has taken hold, submersed in gray
And darken clouds.

I stand and gaze, within the maze,
Numb and cold, which now unfolds,
Body and mind, appear to float, no where
To go, standing alone, no one to hold.

From within the sadden heart, lie the
Fears, which stand apart, as the shallow,
Tears which flow, from the soul, now
Broke and cold.

Stand alone, o' broken soul, for thy love,
Has left thee here, for yet another day, to
Mourn the lost, of sun ray's gone, seeking
Why, you're all alone.

GERALD A. GOTT
17 April 2014

Soul, Life, Dreams

NO PLACE TO RUN

The tempest grows within these walls,
There is no escape, nowhere to run.

My pain, which grows within this fragile
Frame, grows stronger with no place to go.

I walk as if dead, and cold, for this I
Know, within my soul, the day grows short,
And I shall be no more.

What is death, but another life,
Beyond the wall, which is like a
Thin string, how long, I wonder, shall
It hang.

My life is but a vapor, which flees
Like the wind, once passed, never to
Return again.

What is life, but a form of death.
Mockery of life itself, shall never last.
The breath I have, I freely give, but to
Find another.

The sails which I love are out of
Sight, the vessel of no return. The
Day shall come, with no place to run.

GERALD A. GOTT
10 January 1995

UNSPOKEN WORD

Only a word would do,
But no word came, I
Listen again and again.

The years past and no
Word came, as I listen,
Again and again.

Then one day, it was too late,
For the word to be spoken, the
Word, which no one would ever say.

I have grown old, in time, and
Often think, of the word, I
Never heard, and wonder why,
This word, which was never said,
Grew as the void, within my soul.

They're all gone, who never spoke
The word. I cry within, for this
I know, I have trouble speaking this
Word, for which I never heard.

I pray they're in Heaven, where this
Word, is life itself. What is this
Word, which so many fear to speak,
For the shame of man.

The word is soft, as the feathers
Of a dove, the word I seek is love,
For there is, no other.

GERALD A. GOTT
10 January 1995

SOULS ALONE

Alone, beneath the ground I sleep,
For there are many, who look like me,
Beneath the soil of time, that's passed,
Left alone, beneath the grass.

No one cares about the souls,
Which are no longer, around us all.
Upon the quietness, the wind as sound,
We rest alone, beneath the ground.

The stones which mark our last remains,
Stand as sentinals, against the rain.
Reaching up, so ever high, to touch the
Lonely, darken skies. Never to move,
Beneath the moon.

O souls which now, have gone to sleep,
Never to roam, from their peace. For
Time has passed, yet another day,
Beneath the soil, their souls do lay.

The tree limbs stretch, as to embrace,
Yet cannot reach, these souls of clay.
For they have gone on journey's end,
To seek the Master's, gracious hand.

GERALD A. GOTT
19 March 1995

LONELY HOUR

Blood drops fell upon the ground,
As the soldiers stood around, looking
Up at the dying man, whose garment was,
Within their hands.

A piece of cloth, is all he had, as they
Gambled above the sand. The game they
Played, was to their end, for all they
Had, was in their hands.

The lonely soul, with grief, just stared,
Upon the soldiers, whose souls he bared.
If only they would look at me, they would
Know, I am the One, for whom they seek.

For the mocking of the priest, and the jeering
Which is beneath, the cross I bear, is but a tree.
My God, My god, why hast thou forsaken me? Upon
This barren, broken tree. I know my Father, it
Was for thee.

As he cried above the crowd, all eyes looked
Toward the clouds, he alone gave up the ghost,
So no man , could ever boast, for no man took the
Life he had, he gave it up, to the Father's hand.

Darkness fell upon the skies, as the tear drops
Left their eyes, the darken sun, no more to shine.
He has left us, for death has come, for now I know,
That He's the One.

GERALD A. GOTT
27 March 1995

SPIRIT GONE

I often think of days gone by,
Alone each day and every night,
No one to hear my silent cry.

I look around the world about me,
How small I am, how could it be,
That I'm alone, tossed in the sea.

The waves are great, as I'm sucked
Under, they break about, as sounds
Of thunder.

My lifeless form now roams the oceans,
I seek the life, which now is broken.
My spirit drifts as does the currents,
Searching depths of hidden treasures.

Endless is the time I spend, seeking
Life, I cannot win. My spirt's free, once
Embraced by flesh and bone, the vessel
Broken, has no hold.

My spirit's free from mortal bond,
Until the day, my spirit's found. I
Roam the seas, just you and me.

GERALD A. GOTT
10 April 1995

THE PIT

In the pit of mire and decay, my
Soul itself, consumes the day, for
In this pit, of hell I see, no one's
Here, only me.

My cries escape from deep within, and
Yet there's no one, my cries bring in,
Only loneliness and fear I feel, my soul
Cries out into the night, for there is
No one, yet in sight.

This pit of darkness surrounds my soul,
For in this pit, I surely know, the
Hands of death reach out to me, for
My soul, the hands do seek.

I am confused, nowhere to turn, in
This pit, no place to run. I linger
In somber stillness, my only hope of
No return, is death itself, for this
I learn.

GERALD A. GOTT
23 May 1995

SPILLED OUT

The vessel for which I am, can no longer
Hold the grief of sin. My being is
Filled unto the brim, and cannot look, at
Death and sin.

My body's tired and worn, but I remember
What I have sworn, until the end, of time
Itself, my life is nothing, which one has felt.

My piety is for those beneath, for all the hate,
They cannot see, the love I have for all of them,
My grief is great, because of sin.

My burden within, is broken and spilled out,
For all the world, to see the shame, of man, and
What he's done, the shame of hate, towards
The Son.

I ask of thee, forgive their sin, because of fear,
And hate within, their souls shall search, until
The end.

GERALD A. GOTT
19 August 1995

DREAMS

When I was young, I had all day, to
Run around, to laugh, and play. I knew
No worries, nor cares, nor pain, I played
All day, in sun and rain.

Upon the night, when stars are bright, I
Lay upon the pillow's air, and looked into
The empty air.

My eyes close slowly, my mind awake, I
Look forward to another day. In the darkness,
I find myself, searching for the day's which
End, and know tomorrow, it all begins.

Within my slumber, I find a world, for which I
Know not, and all its perils. In the world of
Lifelessness, so real, and yet, without their souls,
For all these people, I do not know.

I awake another day, and remember the night before,
Only glimpses of forms adored, and wondered when, they
Closed the door.

GERALD A. GOTT
30 October 1995

SILENT FALLS

Silently alone I wait, for another
Brutal day, the sea of people, which
Pass me by, I often wonder, who will
Survive.

The sea is endless, with no end in sight,
All different desires, with endless fears,
Throughout the night.

The pain which meets the eyes, with no
Place to hide. The soul melts, within the
Body which it entombs, only to find that
Love, has fled too soon.

Only silence fills the air, for no one speaks,
For grief's despair, eyes look down, upon the
Ground, for all their love, cannot be found.

GERALD A. GOTT
24 December 1995

DARKEN CELL

Night around me, darken twilight's are
Before me, only clouds stand and wait,
Like the rolling, seas of hate.

A ray of hope, is all I know, for I look about
The endless ditch, all I see is hopelessness,
Swallowed up like time itself, never more to
Call for help.

The soul ripped apart, torn asunder, ever more.
In the warp of time itself, lies the answers, in this
Cell.

Only darkness, which abides, conceals the souls, and
Broken pride. Darken cells so void and cold, only darken,
Blacken holes, is all I see, before my soul.

GERALD A. GOTT
4 June 1996

SHATTERED DREAMS

As lightning strikes, and the wind
Howls like madden dogs, I am reminded
Of broken dreams, the lonely years, and
Spring like falls.

Memories bring back, the need of yesterday,
To fill a void, within the inner soul, for only
Yesterdays, can warm the bitter cold.

Through these eyes, of pain, agony, and desolation,
In yesterday's, my soul finds consolation. The game
Of life, goes on for some, for they will never know, the
Lessons learned.

For the sake of love, sacrifices were made, and all I
Have, is yesterday, as the sun appears, with broken
Rays.

GERALD A. GOTT
27 June 1996

WHISPERS IN THE WIND

Silence stands, within the realm, of
Time. For only stars, so far from mine,
Hypnotize the silent mind.

The clouds which stir, in silent winds, you
Hear the whispers, of life itself, for there is
Silence, and nothing else.

Vapors high, deep in the sky, peer far
Above, the naked eye. Only to, cascade to
Earth, to embrace in silent birth.

Whispers, in the wind, we hear, for the
Silence, is so dear, for in silence, we meet
The fear.

Fear of stillness, of time itself, for all we know,
Or ever felt, has passed in time, in silent bliss, we
Ask ourselves, shall we be missed?

GERALD A. GOTT
22 May 1997

O MY SOUL

At last, the joy of ancient days, is before
My eyes, which are of clay. To see the
Beauty, which thou hast made, for all of
This, is but, a day.

Blue green seas, on starless nights,
Within their depths, which have no rest.
Ever present, for one to hold, for at hand,
Is one man's soul.

Star's throughout, the heaven's gate, for all I know,
Has passed away. As the sea, is crystal clear, I find
My soul, is now in fear.

For I see, within my reach, the Vine of Life, which
Thou has preached. Coming forth, with stretch out
Hands, to grasp and hold, this lonely man. Never more,
To weep with shame, for my Lord, has called my name.

In the heaven's, before my eyes, stands the King, in rainbow
Skies. Only Angels, golden harps, fill the air, which stir's our
Hearts. Joyful sounds of praise indeed, fills' the air, and
Strengthen's me.

For the Master, with loving eyes, gather's us, to His side. Unto
Thee, my Lord and King, our voices rise, in Heaven's realm, glory
Be, to thee alone.

GERALD A. GOTT
25 August 1998

THE BOOK

Old and torn, from years of scorn, lies
The truth, within these pages, for only
Truth, survived the ages.

Works of old, beyond the years, as countless
Souls, began to fear, for death itself, was standing
Near. But within, these lifeless pages, death was
Conquered, by love alone, for which these pages,
Have surely shown.

Cracked and worn, with prints of hunger, lies the
Proof, of one which wondered. Life itself, has just
Appeared, between these pages, which are so dear.

Soiled by tears, of broken hearts, spotted sheets, now
Torn apart. Held together, by tape now gone, for time
Itself, has finally won.

But in the Book, forever stands, the words of life, for
Every man. Broken souls, of no tomorrow's, falls upon
This Book of sorrows.

For within, are hidden secrets, for mortal
Souls, which search its depths, the life they
Seek, their soul's have met.

GERALD A. GOTT
7 January 1999

SPIRIT'S BROKEN

Grieve not the heart, that has not gone, but hold to
Love, which thou hast found. For in time, love will hold
Those things which are, the souls of those, who
Now have past.

Lonely hills surround time itself, never ending whispers,
Of joys now seen, only love itself, upon the scene,
Times of laughter, joy and fun, for all have gone, where time begun.

Broken spirit's searching time, for past joys, never found. Endless
Echo's, broken soul's, only time, itself will know, why the spirit's, in
Solace blamed, shall always hurt, because of shame.

Broken spirit's, grieve not the day, for all have gone, in time away. For
All shall gather, in lonely hills, to chase the spirit's, and not be still. Sadness
Falls upon the land, for all the spirit's, which shall be called, will enter
Darkness, with weeping tears, for time has won, their soul's in fear.

Utter darkness surrounds them all, for their crying which no one hears, falls
Upon the darken void, endless echo's as sounding brass, can't be heard,
from
Soul's now past.

GERALD A. GOTT
2 February 2000

TORN WITHIN

Within my soul, of lifeless breath, is
Darkness hidden, where no one slept. Gripping
Hold with strength of iron, will not loosen,
Before the fire.

Screeching screams of fear and dread, for there
Is no one, which tears will shed. From the depths,
Of hell itself, my heart now tears, my soul apart.

For the darkness, consumes my soul, upon the flesh,
Of rotten bones, decay of life, of souls of joy, forever lost,
Forever sorry.

Demons which conquered, my soul within, came from the
Depths, of darken walls and damp domains, for only death,
Shall remain.

Love of many, wilt like rain, for the demons, bring
Only pain. Lonely eyes, which search the realm, to find that,
Darken skies prevail.

O' my soul, of pain and grief, search within the darken pit,
For rays of light, which can't exist, only darkness shall remain,
Within the pit, of death and pain.

GERALD A. GOTT
5 February 2002

WHISPERS NOT

Whisper not, which silence cannot hear, for within
The wind, comes stillness, yet not long, for within
My soul, does light appear.

Only closeness, can grasp the sounds, which
Drop upon the dampened ground. For one soul,
Cry's to another, hear not what I say, for my
Soul shall rest today.

Many years, of restless silence, for no soul,
Would dare to hear, the pain within the sphere,
For life itself, no longer dear.

For only man, can say within, for I am
Weak, and thou art strong, whisper not within the
Wind, for only silence, has now began.

GERALD A. GOTT
15 March 2005

LIFELESS SOULS

Upon my journey of life, I have but
Observed, the souls of men, who
Live, but know not, their plight.

Where's the Light, which came upon
This earth? For man saw
The Light, denied the living deity,
Before them.

How sad to live, and die within, for
Darkness only knows darkness, for the
Light, which would shine within, is held
At bay, for only man, if thou would sway.

Lifeless soul's of no return, for the Light,
Which you did spurn, shall consume
You, and thou shall burn.

For the love, of One who came, cried within
For all the pain, which He endured. For man
Alone, has denied, the love of God, and why
He died.

Now lifeless soul's, of no return, must forever
Search, within the night, for the day, in which they
Die, lifeless soul's begin to cry.

GERALD A. GOTT
April 11, 2005

TRAIL OF TEARS

Along the heartless silent walk, stillness
Prevails with every breath, knowing not
When struck with death.

Hunger and pain taking its toll, as each
One who walks alone, their soul now searching,
Along the way, seeking the heavens, as they pray.

Once were proud and mighty in strength, fall
Upon the dampen ground, only to find, there
Was no sound. No sound of life, of joy and tears,
For only now, lies the fear.

Broken souls marching forward, knowing not
The time nor day, the march would end, and life
Itself, would begin. Afresh and new, with fear behind,
With death held captive, no longer seeking the
Weakened souls, for death itself, no longer holds

GERALD A. GOTT
16 October 2013

MOURN

The day is cloudy, with very little sun,
For the field, of lonely souls await the
Solemn form of no return.

No one there, but the gravedigger's hole,
A lonely casket, waits for someone to show.
Where is the sorrow, for the form inside, no
One is there, no place to hide.

The life is now gone, the figure is dead, for
Darkness now falls, on casket and form, for
Nothing has changed, for life must go on.

The field of souls has taken another, to
Lie among them, in silent tribute, to life which
Was, now hidden below, from rain and thunder.

GERALD A. GOTT
25 November 2013

VOICES

Voices heard, no one hears, always
Swaying with the fear. For in the light,
In blinding sight, are the piercing, sounds
Of fright.

Longing for the silent bliss, never reaching
In the mist, for the fear, it shall be missed.
Days on end, troubled waters just ahead, why
The hell, get out of bed?

Another day in silent scorn, why is the heart,
So ripped and torn? Broken pieces lie around, no
One caring if they're found. Another day upon
The sill, why is the heart, so cold and still?

Passing within the light, the dead like
Creature passes by, clinging on, that one day
Soon, it's soul shall pass, before the moon.

GERALD A. GOTT
28 January 2014

BROKEN TEARS

Within the air, in which they fall,
No one can hear, their silent call,
For in the broken, sphere's of pain,
The soul is crushed, as endless rain.

The sound of sadness, lasting night's,
Casting crystals before the light,
Gleaming sorrow, within our sight.

No sound nor touch, relieve the stream,
Only darkness, with dread despair, hopeless
Sorrow, for no one's there.

As the endless, tear drops fall, the world
Has ended, life has stalled, as if now frozen,
Within the sphere, the tears are silent, and
Clinging near.

Clinging to the soul released, unto the body,
Which lies beneath, silence finds a resting
Place, for broken hearts, another day.

GERALD A. GOTT
3 July 2014

ETERNAL LIGHT

Total darkness, which hides within,
Walking blindly, before the wind, for
In the world, we captured sin.

Looking not before our eyes, at the
Light, beside our side, ever waiting for
Our soul's, to grasp the light, and forever
Hold.

Only man with open eye's, darken soul's,
Beneath the skies, seek the darkness, which
Abides, ever watching, deep inside.

O' the peace, which never comes, due to
Soul's, forever run, seeking what is not,
So near, always hiding, due to fear.

Eternal light, standing by, for one soul,
To see and cry, take me from this darken
Void, which has hold, and crushed the joy.

Than the light, with tender hands, lift the
Soul, from barren lands, giving life where
None was found, for only beauty, which
Now abounds.

GERALD A. GOTT
9 June 2014

MISTY GRAY

Within the fog, so dense and thick,
Lies the blindness, that one can't
Miss. For the eye can only see, the
Path before it, beneath their feet.

Fear abounds, in darken folds, before
The gray, had taken hold. Within the mist,
Of silent sounds, the eye's keep searching,
For light not found.

Eerie are the fold's of gray, just ahead,
Before the day, for in blindness, fear
Succumbs, to emotions, which now are numb.

Fear itself, grips the soul, knowing not for
What it holds, before the eye's, in wrenching
Pain, blinding madness, begins to gain.

Now in darkness, light unfolds, as the fear,
Begins to fade, for the gray's, another shade.
Light before the lonely souls, giving hope,
Upon the shore.

GERALD A. GOTT
2 August 2014

ALONG THE ROAD

Upon the road of life, I was free,
The world in sight, the road was
Smooth, as if on ice. No bumps when
Life began, time came fast, like grains
Of sand.

Over year's, which came so fast, I stand
And look, which now has past, the good
And bad, which never last.

The soften hearts, and tears which fell,
Are all now gone, no one to tell. Silent
Time's which now abound, I find myself,
Wondering why, I now can hear, their
Silent cry.

Along the road, of life itself, filled with
Sand, and holes to fill, I step aside, with
Gentle ease, seeing other's, in stride with me.

GERALD A. GOTT
12 December 2014

TEARS IN THE WIND

Crying soul within the wind, broken
Heart in time will mend, for now the
Tears, which flow, with no control,
Must reach the heaven's, portal gates,
Upon the wind, they leave in hast.

O' the scream, which leaves the lips,
From the depths, sounds of anguish,
Mixed with fear, brings the truth, so
Very near.

As the vapors, reach the sky, the vacant
Look, upon the eye, seeking answers, for
There's none, only silence, beneath the sun.
As the crystals, fall so near, for the one,
We held so dear.

So the wind, in force of one, take's the sorrow,
Which leave's us numb, to a place, of light and
Grace, far above the wretched race.

GERALD A. GOTT
24 Decemeber 2014

Time

VAPOR OF TIME

My life is but a vapor, it's
Like the print upon the paper,
One day my life is great, the
Next, as if I'm dead.

I spend the day knowing the pain,
And yet in time, within my mind, I
Sense the dread, of another day.

The dark clouds seem to encase
My soul, and yet the rays of sunlight,
Which breaks forth, gives a hint of
Happier times of days of old.

When I was young, I had all the time
To run and play, and now I know, time
Itself stands still for no one, for the time
I see, has finally come.

GERALD A. GOTT
30 June 1995

ENDLESS TIME

I cry aloud, with no response, to
Voiceless echoes, of no return, to
Only hear, my voice interned.

Reaching for, the sound of time, obtaining
Only, what is mine. To the ear, the music
Flows, upon the sharpest, clearest note.

Brain waves flutter, pressed by tone, for the
Sounds, can only hold, the nerves within, alas
Will break, upon the notes, this silent day.

Within the realm, of solemn notes, there is a
Tune, which seems to flow,upon the wind,
Of no return, voices, which no one heard.

Endless as my eyes can see, the silent sounds,
Now run and creep, as the pearls, of rain drops
Fall, the open notes, are closed to all.

GERALD A. GOTT
21 October 1996

SWEET HOUR

When time alone, does not vanish, for at
The hour, my soul is famished, alone at
Last, my spirit filled, my soul shall rest,
No longer stilled.

Within the hour, thy ears alone, I seek to
Listen, to seek thy throne, for only you, have
Truely known.

The world about me, is like the sea, to swim
Forever, and never meet, the one I called for, in
Darkness past, for all the world, has come at last.

Overcome by time itself, my soul is vexed, which
Time has dealt, the open wounds, no more to heal,
The time is now, for me to kneel.

AS the hour, draws to an end, upon thy throne, I
Cast my sins, thy wings which close, around thy
Throne, shall catch and hold, my very soul.

GERALD A. GOTT
14 January 1996

TRAGIC

Years have passed, as leaves from a
Tree, old withered hands, and bony
Old knees, is all time has left, upon
These old bones, waiting for death.

Eyes which have seen, the beauty of
Time, look upon scenes, no longer are
Mine.

The mind, which was sharp, appears a
Bit dim, often wondering, in times of the
Past, and often not here. Asking oneself,
Where has time disappeared.

Alive, so alive, and yet dead, for time slipped
Away, with laughter and tears, for time has
Returned, where time was so dear.

GERALD A. GOTT
25 June 1996

VAST DOMAIN

Time about to explode, like a grenade, to
Pull the pin, and let it go. The flash of light,
Brightens the skies, for all around, shall
Surely die.

To feel the pain, and hear their screams, would
Cause the grief, inside to flee. No where to run,
No where to hide, for all about me, scream and
Cry.

For death is here, and will not leave, for death
Itself, shall never flee. In the hands of death's domain,
Souls have wandered, through grief and pain.

Endless seas of searching souls, seeking, vengeance, with
No place to go. Only time which does not end, will meet
These souls, where they began.

Endless walls, of blue and stars, shall meet us all, when
Angels call.

GERALD A. GOTT
29 June 1996

SILENT ETERNITY

As time around me, appears so dim, I
Often wonder, where will it end, one day
At last, my soul is gone, and time itself, is
Like a song.

When did it start, where will it end, for time
Alone, shall always stand. Silently sipping
Away from man, the time he needs, has always
Been.

The skies as blue, as oceans deep, for eternity, thy
Soul shall weep, upon the depths, of no return, the
Flames of hell, forever burn.

Silently, eternity waits, for time itself, is like the day,
Ever long, with time to spare, until the stars, enclose
The snare.

GERALD A. GOTT
7 January 1997

FAREWELL

It's time to say good-bye, and yet I wonder why,
For time itself, has slipped away, I have not,
Another day.

Echoes of distant sounds, fall lifeless, upon the
Ground, absorbing only silent cries, for only echoes,
Are heard tonight.

The longing heart, with grief as dressing, silence is
The only blessing. Where did it go, I do not know,
For in the shadows, the soul bemoans, for in the
Dressing, there are no blessings.

Now is the time, of no return, sands as the crystals,
Which fall from heaven, leaves the imprint, of one
Now missed.

GERALD A. GOTT
1 March 1997

FOOT STEPS

Travel as the sun rises, in time,
There are no surprises. Only
Eternity of silent stills, which appear
As distant hills.

Looking back, in time itself, brings
Painful thoughts, which time has brought.
Reaching ahead, just beyond the bend, for
Life has gone, where I have been.

Foot steps follow, within my wake, for fear
Itself, does not quake, fear alone, has brought
But hate, for time has passed, and left this fate.

For all I knew, and loved in life, has vanished,
And left me blind. Foot steps in, the distant hills,
Can only bring, the love, which fills.

Reaching out, as to unfold, to touch this lost, and
Silent soul.

GERALD A. GOTT
12 June 1997

DESPAIR IN TIME

Darkness, before the eyes of time, knowing
Not when reapers chime, for the earth, has
Claimed you mine.

Joys of days, now gone by, for now they hear,
But solemn cries. Brightness gone, like stars which
Hide, for their brightness, in death, has died.

Suffered old, in time itself, weary from, the battles fought,
Only time, with scars have brought, remain in sight, for
Naked eyes. Bulging sockets unaware, for the eyes, in darkness
Stare.

Silence, engulfs the mind, eternity waits, holding but, the trails
Of time. Darken walls, of silent whispers, claim the soul, no longer
With us.

GERALD A. GOTT
5 August 1997

DENIED

Surrounded by sightless sounds, of
Crying depths of despair, clinging to
The rim of life.

For in the realm, of man alone, stands
Decay of time itself. For thy love, which
Suffered so, could only reach, and bestow,
The gift of life, which man denied.

Reaching out, with broken heart, for man again,
In blinding furry, took the One, who gave them
Life, for all could see, it's hate that blinds.

With stricken soul, now washed away, the Father
Watches, with sadden eyes, for all you hear, is
Man's own lies.

Man with Pride, and fear inside, took the One,
They knew would die.

Empty now of despair, the world goes on, without a care.
For man alone, shall seek one day, the One they placed, within
This grave.

GERALD A. GOTT
22 January 1998

ENDLESS SAND

As time evaporates, the endless strands,
Only to come back, where it all began, to
Find the place, where I now stand.

Regrests abound, forgiveness not found, within
The strands, of endless sand. The heart knows
Well, the hidden shame, for with the sand, the
Darkness came.

Darkness will, forever stand, upon the soul, now
Gone, and damned. Within the darken flames, which
Only death can see, lies the souls, of many, upon the
Broken sea.

Surrounded by, the depths of death, only cursing with
Regret, forge past, the darken flames, only souls, which
Have no light, forever shall remain.

Returning sands, of wonder years, return again, with other
Strands, to form the faith, of sinful man.

GERALD A. GOTT
10 March 1998

SPIRAL INTO SILENCE

Being aware of time, which no longer
Waits for man, for no one came, for
They were scared. Twinkling within, has
No meaning, emptiness is the only survivor.

To plea, for just one moment, but please go
Unanswered, for fear abounds, where is courage?
Fear has conquered, and left the brave, faint.

To reach and grasp, the sword of courage, for time
Has dealt a deadly blow. For the survivor, has many
Victories, but the gleam, in the hunter's eye, has none.

Void is not to have, courage cannot be found, only
Fear remains, for the soul of man, has melted, as candles
Upon the deck.

Out to sea, with sails full blown, if only man, would have
Known. But little remains, of prideful man, for in victory,
They are, but sand. Like the crystals, within the sky, the
Only choice, has surely died.

GERALD A. GOTT
1 April 1998

YESTERDAY

Upon the time, when I was young, for the
Days, have just begun. Always vibrant, youthful
Strength, never tiring, never meek.

Seeking for adventures fold, to unleash, its deadly
Hold. Searching for, the new day sun, acting silly,
Having fun.

Dusk arrives, with Autumn leaves, falling down amid
The trees, chilly winds, surrounds the soul, for the moon,
Has brought the cold.

These are days and nights gone past, for the years, which never
Last, have arrived upon the scene, to take away, the youthful gleam.
Days of old, which seemed so real, for only age, did time now steal.

Yesterday when I was young, for now I know, where it begun. Ageless
Soul of youthful days, for I look back, and could not stay. Time has
Come, to take my soul, on journey's end, where no one knows.

But the King, which gave me life, stands above, before the light.
Waiting for this ageless soul, to come before, the Saviour's Throne. With
Out reached arms, He grasp my hand, and leads me to, the promised land.

GERALD A. GOTT
1 November 1998

TIME ITSELF

Silent moments with no sound, for time is by me, all around
Which can't be found. Seeking just beyond the blue, finding no one,
Especially you. Far in the distance, a shadow stands motionless,
Searching for nearness, if time allows.

But time continues its journey, through ever thickening clouds, as
Eyes and hearts, seek our journey's end, only to find out, time
Itself, is not the sin.

O' to touch, the past now hidden, only memories in touch, with
Time, holds the secret, which is not mine. For sweetness ends, with
Bitter blight, far into the silent night.

Darkness surrounds the lonely form, in silent depths of grief and
Pain, for time itself, has passed again. Awaken soul and see the
Day, casting darkness along the way.

GERALD A. GOTT
23 August 2013

ONLY TIME

Only time is like the wind, in ageless
Past which time forgot, the age of man,
Has never stopped.

In the cradle, with eyes wide open, seeing
Beauty before the fall, O the wonder of
It all.

Through the years, as time flies by, we
Find ourselves, asking why. I've just begun
My journey's in, and forgot when it all began.

Age has finally won the race, my body's old
And losing pace, the aches and pains which fill
My soul, for death itself, beyond my reach, always
There, so we can meet.

GERALD A. GOTT
10 October 2013

SIMPLE TIMES

Looking back into the past, I
See the good, which time had
Cast. The simple life, we never
Thought would pass.

Never knowing another day, would
Come or go, and never stay. The simple
Life of leisure time, no hurry or rush, and
Wonder why, all the fuss.

The joy of blooming flowers, always
Looking for sprint time showers. Casting
Eyes upon the sparrows, never worrying
About tomorrow.

Simple times have passed us by, never knowing
The reason why. Now it's hurry, hurry, while
All the time, there's all the stress, with all
The worry.

O' to have the simple times, which have come
And gone, and passed us by.

GERALD A. GOTT
1 November 2013

LONELY HOUR

Seeking wonders within the blue,
Darken skies with cloudy hue. Only
Silence meets the ear, for no figures,
Have appeared.

Have I survived to be alone, or is it that,
They must not have shown? Coming from the mist
Ashore, lonely souls forever more. Seeking
Solace from the pain, for only silence, appears
To reign.

Lonely hour, which seeks my life, for I fear I
Cannot hide, only time will tell my faith, for
Now I seek, another way.

For I know within my soul, this day and hour,
Has been foretold, for silence stands within
The sphere, knowing all souls, await to hear.

Lonely hour which stands alone, waiting again
For a solemn soul, seeking a sound of life anew,
O' to hear, the sound they knew.

Alone around me, within the mist, I cannot hear,
The souls amiss, for they like me, stand alone in
Silent bliss.

GERALD A. GOTT
2 November 2013

PRESENT TIME

One never thinks, of time left behind, for only
The future, is before their eyes. Events which
Will follow, their lives through time itself.

No worry of mind, for there is always tomorrow,
Not knowing what waits, nor caring to share, for
They're in a hurry, going somewhere.

As we hustle in our busy lives, never seeing what's
Before our eyes, the beauty lies before us, always
There as foretold by time.

As we look and ask, why the blur before my eyes,
For there is something I left behind. Never knowing
The reason why, we missed the beauty before our
Eyes.

Time has taken our pace away, slowed us down
Another day, see the beauty before our eyes, and
Wonder why, we never cried.

Tear drops fall upon the ground, landing softly
With little sound, knowing now the reason why,
Our life alone, stands still in time.

GERALD A. GOTT
7 December 2013

NO MORE

O' to see, and feel the breeze, feel the
Warmth, upon my face, from the sun, so
Far away, only darkness surrounds my
Soul, only dampness filled with cold, awaits
My eyes forever closed.

For in the vault, lid sealed tight, I sense a
Loneliness, filled with fright, knowing not that
Time has gone, leaving me, but all alone.

Lying just beyond the ground, no one knowing,
Nor hear the sounds, of souls now under, this
Very ground. Happy laughter so far away, I swear
I heard this very day.

Time has come, the end at last, and yet I know, how
Wide and vast, time itself has always been, for now
I know, when time began.

Only darkness shields my emotion, for there is no one,
Who truly knows, these lonely walls, which hide my
Soul.

GERALD A. GOTT
26 December 2013

SILENT TIMES

Silent times are in the wind, blowing
Fury in sight of man, only hatred now
Abides, casting pain, no place to hide.

Seeking solace which can't be found,
Longing peace, within the stillness,
Only sadness, now abounds.

Hear the cries, within the wind, for
The souls, have cast their sins, upon
The clouds, which now have dimmed.

Ever more, in darken clouds, moving
Forward, in the shroud, have moved
About, leaving bodies, which can't
Be found.

Now the souls, have found the peace,
Which man has sought, for many years,
For in this place, there are no tears.

GERALD A. GOTT
22 July 2014

Inner self and Friendship

SERENE

In the silence of the night, by the
Twilight of the skies, silence heard
By stars above, and the ones we
Truly love.

Reach toward the silent realm, reach towards
The endless void, for no man can obtain, the
Emptiness within its frame.

Silent waves, which break above, only sound
Eternal love. Darkness falls upon one's soul,
For in darkness, no one knows, all the pain,
Which seems to grow, upon the everlasting soul.

Silence is the sound of life, and in silence,
One will die. Only death, which sits and waits,
For there is yet, another day, for the silence, to
Take its shape.

In the realm of no return, silence will forever
Burn. Burn upon the souls of men, never more will
One depend, upon the silence, which never ends.

GERALD A. GOTT
7 September 1993

FALLING CRYSTALS

From within the bowels I form,
In time, I rest dormant, and
Cling in side.

I am crystal clear, with no
Substance in which to draw from.
I travel from the soul of man,
And die.

My grief is great, the pain
Never ending. I have but one
Purpose in life, to bring sorrow,
For those within my sight.

My travel may never come, but
For many, I have come and gone.
To their bewilderment, I fall
Like leaves upon the ground.

I see the light, just beyond the
Eye, this is where, I shall die.
As I fall, with no sound, the
Crystals split, and fall around.

The heavens open, and takes them
In, no more to fall, on empty winds.

GERALD A. GOTT
31 January 1995

SILENT TEARS

I cry aloud, and no one hears, for
In my soul, which is so near, the
Tear drops fall, in silent pain, just
   As the dew, turns into rain.

For deep inside, this darken cell,
There lives a pain that cannot dwell,
The grief so great, it damn's the day,
   For in the end, my soul shall pay.

In silence, I shall play the fool, until
One day, which will be soon, my soul
Shall weep, until the spring, for in this
Time, my life shall bring, the end of time,
   My soul decays.

GERALD A. GOTT
16 June 1995

FROM WITHOUT

In the garden from which I was, I
Now gaze, beyond the haze. The
Peace and tranquility for which I had,
I find no longer, in upon the land.

The beauty of the foliage upon the trees,
I no longer find, within these weeds. Thorns,
And thistles, is all I have, because of sin,
O' how sad.

I talked with God almost every day, and now
I feel as if I'm clay, to work the fields and hills
Each day.

I named the animals of all the land, I had them
All within my hands, to touch and love with all
My heart, and now I'm told, to depart.

I see the beauty from far away, I remember that
Faithful day, for when I took of that forbidden
Fruit, I learned the awful bitter truth.

I should have listen to God's still voice, you
Had all that I could give, which you have lost
Because of sin.

GERALD A. GOTT
2 July 1995

SOLITUDE

In the solitude of time I spend,
Listening for the sounds of sin,
For they elude me every day, for
This I know, I will surely pay.

The beauty of the time has past,
What awaits me, has come at last.
As the raindrops soak the ground,
My love has lasted, proven sound.

As the chimes ring their song, I
No longer feel belonged, for as time
Has passed me by, I for one, shall surely die.

GERALD A. GOTT
4 July 1995

TEARS UPON THE PILLOW

The golden hair, which flows like clouds,
Upon the skies, my heart is broken, I wonder
Why. All the hurt which I have caused, I see
Upon, the pillow fall.

The body shakes, the pain is clear, and yet I
Know, to not come near, for in the pain for
Which I see, I know it's due because of me.

The comfort, which I try to bring, is like the
Desert, without the rain, dry and parched,
Which causes pain.

Tears fall from swollen eyes, caused by pain
From deep inside. I touch the body, which
Sleeps for now, and say I'm sorry, for this
I vow, never more shall thy tears fall, because
Of me, I pray the Lord, my soul to keep.

GERALD A. GOTT
31 July 1995

TAPS

As rain drops fall, upon the ground,
Through the granite, no sound is found,
As moisture is, a part of life, none is
Found, not even mine.

Morning breaks, sun rays bright,
Dew drops wet, from early night. Stillness
As, the breath can see, tombstones encase
The old, oak tree.

Sounds which break, into the air, can only bring
With it despair, the solemn tune, which passes
By, upon the sound, for all to cry.

Into the skies, into the wind, the only sounds,
Which cannot win, the hearts of those, who are
Beneath, for in their sorrow, no soul shall breathe.

As the bugle, in case, is closed, upon the casket,
A lonely rose, stands alone in sunlight skies, to
Die again, this lonely night.

GERALD A. GOTT
1 September 1995

TEARS UPON STONES

The granite's cry into the night, into the
Air of no return, the cries go out, no one
Concerned.

Upon the stone's the dew drops rest, beneath
The ground, thy soul to cast. No more to laugh,
And run, and play, the one I love, is gone today.

The time of joy, no more is found, for all I loved,
Is underground. I sit and wait, and linger on, for
One day soon, just like the song, the end will come,
And take away, my soul, this lonely, forgotten day.

In the stillness of the night, the moonlight glistens,
From their sides, for there is no one, yet in sight

The sun breaks early, amidst the dew, on a hillside,
Stands a few, who look with wonder, upon the sight,
For the granite's, cried last night.

GERALD A. GOTT
27 October 1995

SEARCHING

With each awaking day, my life
Clings as if by clay, never separating
From within itself, only binding, with
Time as substance, holding nerves and
Heart, as breath draws near.

In the depts of the soul of man, there
Lies a place, as desolate as barren land.
For no life exists, nor can abide, for all to
Enter, shall surely die.

As the currents flow underneath, the ills of
Man for all to see, to search within, and find
Them not, for only time, has not forgot.

The searching soul, the seeking eyes, search the
Land, and endless skies, to find the thing, which
Longs to hide.

GERALD A. GOTT
1 January 1996

MADNESS

The only sound, which can be found,
Is but the rustle, of foliage near, for in
The evergreen, the eyes appear.

Distant stares of darken dreams, within
The eyes, I feel their fear, damning all
Who might, come near.

For the touch, of human hands, claims the
Soul, within the sand. Empty minds have gone
Mad, for the death, of one is sad.

The eyes are focused, searching, seeking, their
Hopeless sounds, for all their cries, reach
Underground, for this is where, their souls are bound.

For the faint, and weary dread, the eyes and sounds,
Of souls, now dead. Upon the rock, of steel and bone,
Stands the fear, which man has shown. This is where,
The eyes just stare.

GERALD A. GOTT
23 January 1996

THE ROOM

Around they sat, and heard the sound, the
Voice rang out, and sadness found, its way
Through laughter, smiles, and tears.

The noise of anger, frustration, fears, all
Seem to stop, and disappear. The voice rang
Out, stopping here and there, not because of
Breath, but because of tears.

Within the room, no sound was heard, silence
Took hold, as the words were spoke, to the ears
Of those within the walls, a solemn note, for reality
Had crept in, with memories of the past.

The sudden realization, appeared within a flash, for
All within the room, knew it wouldn't last. The
Grief poured out, unto the very end, and when it
Was all over, all the tears, appear to blend.

Words were spoken, true as day, for life's sorrows,
Appear that way. Upon the floor, of the empty room,
Lies the heartaches, grief, and gloom.

GERALD A. GOTT
27 March 1996

DEPTHS OF MAN

Depths of man, of shame and hate,
For their pride, they can't relate, all
Is dead before their wake.

Bodies tossed and souls consumed,
For man is seeking, something new.
Never pleased, with what ne has, always
Searching, always mad.

Joy of love has fled away, due to man and
All his hate. For the love, that man once had,
Is covered up, with greed and pride, for there is
No place, for man to hide.

Only darken souls remain, for the hate, has left a
Stain, for depths of man again, has stole the
Love, and left the pain.

GERALD A. GOTT
9 June 1996

THE GROUP

Alone they sat, with arms upon
Their laps, peering at one another,
Wanting not to speak, for fear of
Voiceless souls, hidden like roaring
Thunder.

One spoke and you, could feel the pain,
The sliver of steel, pierced deep within, that
Lonely soul. Faces glared across the room,
For no one dared to move.

One small voice, began its distant cry, the voice
Itself, seemed to stand, before their eyes, the voice
So small and frail, disappeared as melting snow,
Among the hardened hail.

Why the grief, with all its pain, appears before us,
Like fallen rain? For all the souls, within the group,
Have all been scarred, like preying bears, for all to shoot.

As the souls bleed, and seek each other, the distant
Voice, is heard like thunder, the plea of life, surrounds
Us all, with empty hands, and broken hearts, the group
Stands up, and then departs.

GERALD A. GOTT
16 June 1996

NO OTHER

In times of solitude, and grief, I
Seek thy name, for there is no other,
For whom I call, will always hear, even
Though I cry in fear.

Within the hearts of all mankind, no other
Knows, the pain I hide, for deep within this
Very soul, I cry aloud, to Him who knows.

Depressed of mind, I find the body's, old inside.
All I loved, is gone away, as tired old eyes, peer
Through the haze.

No other, in the realm of time, has always heard, my
Silent cry, for He alone, is always there, to hear my
Cry and pleading prayer.

NO other has the love and grace, to which I seek, to
See His face. Upon my death, I leave behind, the shell
Which He, so kindly bind, for all the years, I lived inside,
He was there, to hear my cries.

GERALD A. GOTT
1 July 1996

THE FLAG

I once was the pride of the Nation, for
In time of peace, I was looked upon as
The symbol of the country.

I flew over many battles far beneath my
Border, saw the agony, pain, and blood, as
Eyes looked upon my colors.

I once was the symbol of strength and might,
But now I"m spit upon, cursed, and burned,
They say they have a right to hate me, for the
Things which I have done, but I have offended
No one, In this country, which I love.

I still fly high above the blessed ground, and
Know one day, I will not be found. For my
Colors are fading, along with all my strengths,
For the people have hasten, my fall they surely
Bring.

GERALD A.GOTT
26 November 1996

QUIET SPACE

Listen to the silent winds, feel the
Freshness, from within. Empty eyes
Searching round, silent winds upon the ground.

Void of motion, no one thought, brought
The silence, filled with tears, consumed by
Stars, and human fears.

Rustling neath, leave's anew, for the sorrow,
Filled with pain, prick's the heart, of man again.
Silent winds passing by, for only man, to wonder why.

Edge of darkness, reached my soul, silent wails, of pain and
Grief, in the darkness, only meet, for the tears, which fall
Outside, cleanses pain, I try to hide.

Silent winds, and empty clouds, stand amist, the silent
Crowd. Ashes to, the caring winds, where the souls, have
Cast, their sins.

GERALD A. GOTT
10 September 1997

FRIEND

Only you, would stand so near, for all the
Others, have left in fear. For all the laughter,
And pain we shared, no other friend, I count so dear.

Knowing weakness and sullen times, you my friend,
Could always find. Listen to my tales of woe, and never
Ask, for me to go.

Times apart, and times so near, for only we, knew all
Our fears. Never wanting to tell it all, for my friend, it's
You, I called.

Our hearts were broken, in times which passed, and yet, we
Had, the bond, which last. A bond so strong, within the
Times, no man could break, for the twine.

Now death has come, and taken all, for all the years, we
Shared our thoughts, and now my friend, time has brought,
Another chapter in our lives, for one of us, will leave tonight.

Farewell my friend, for I must go, and when we meet, again
In time, you're sure to hear, my call again, and recognize the
Voice now gone, to grasp the hand, within the skies, and
Greet each other, a'mist the Light.

GERALD A. GOTT
2 June 1998

SORROWS

Sorrows upon the rocks, for no other,
Can search the sea, for only sadness,
Is here, you see.

Broken limbs, which cannot mend, fall
About, upon the rocks, which cannot hide.
For only bed's, of pearl await, beneath the
Ties, of rage and hate.

Succumb by torments, forever known, silent
Souls, can now be shown. Within the silence,
Which prevails silent souls, are now unveiled.

With all the world, to see their shame, and wonder
Why, their souls, aren't claimed. Broken limbs, with
Sullen stares, upon the rocks, of despair, reaching out
For souls to claim, the broken limbs, which now, remain.

Upon the rocks, of despair, there is no one, around to share.
The shattered dreams, of fallen souls, for which the eye, in
Glimmering light, will search for souls, on silent nights.

GERALD A. GOTT
20 June 1998

INTRUDER

Taken by surprise, this night, I find
Within, no strength to fight. For I know,
My struggle's great, my despairing mind, is
Seeking grace.

This intruder, within my soul, seems for now,
To have control. How I hate, this curse I have,
For now I know, the darken ways, for my soul,
In dark dismay, shall surely fall, and curse my day.

Consumed within, by darken walls, I find that
One, will hear my call. For He alone, will know
My fear, and He alone, will always hear.

The fight continues, within my soul, for darken walls of
Strength's unknown, against the soul, which seems alone.
Awaits to hear, from heaven's gate, darken soul, of eternal
Hate, leave this soul, come not this way.

Within the tattered, soul which stands, now healed by hands,
Not seen by man, within the realm, of Angels' feet, below
His throne, is where they meet.

GERALD A. GOTT
21 June 1998

BROKEN SPIRITS

Grieve not the heart, that has not gone, but hold to the
Love, which thou has found. Caught in time,the souls of those,
Which man can't hold.

Lonely hills surround time itself, never ending whispers, of
Joys now past. Times of laughter, joy and fun, for all have gone,
And sadly shunned.

Broken spirit's searching time, endless echo's, broken soul's,
Only time, itself will know, why the spirit's, in silent frames,
Shall always hurt, because of shame.

Broken spirit's, grieve not the day, for all have gone, in time away. For
All shall gather, on lonely hills, to chase the spirit's, that can't be still.
Sadness
Falls upon the land, for all the spirit's, entering darkness, with
Weeping tears, for time has won, their soul's in fear.

Broken spirits are like the spray, of ocean's depths, upon its prey,
Drowning out the cry of night, their souls are lost, and hid from sight.
Roaming earth, and skies alike, broken spirits, have taken flight.

GERALD A. GOTT
11 November 2000

SHADOW IN THE WIND

Who am I? But a shadow in the wind, casting
Light which time has dimmed. Seeing through
Faulty vales, for time itself, have never failed.

Alone as if, I just arrived, and yet I know, my
Soul shall hide. Seeing wonders before my eyes.
Seeking first, the shining Light.

For He alone created life, from the dust, beneath
The skies. Giving man a living soul, to search
The heavens, that he might know, that God Himself,
Is not alone.

I am but, a man of clay, which God alone, did create.
For He died a sinless death, that I myself, might have
Breath.

From clay, to man in just one day, for God alone,
Shall be my stay. My soul shall find, that shining
Light, with open arms, O' what delight.

GERALD A. GOTT
11 October 2001

ETERNAL CRY

Covered by the darken realm, which in
Turn, sheds no light, for the cries, of those
Beneath, seek the solace, of eternal peace.

Far within, their cries are heard, but only
By, the one entomb. They alone, can only
Hear, the cry of those, in hopeless fear.

Tears which filled, the darken abyss, shall
Never, in their flight, fall upon the Holy
Light. Gnashing teeth, in pain is heard,
Never more to hear, the Word.

Casting out, beyond the stars, wounded souls
With lasting scars, forever parted, without hope,
From the Light, they did not know.

Angel's weeping, from clouds on high, for
They hear, the wounded cry, searching, pleading,
For just one glimpse, of the One, which God had
Sent. Who shed His blood, for those of sin, always
Feeling, the pain again.

GERALD A. GOTT
26 January 2003

SOMEWHERE IN THE NIGHT

I look around, I wonder why, there stands
No one, before my eyes. I reach to touch,
But cannot find, the one I have, upon my
Mind.

Within my soul, I search for fire, to find that
I, have no desire. Knowing that, my life is ending,
For time has passed, and left me standing.

Within the silence, of the night, the stars appear,
The moon shown bright, the brighten color, of moon
Night glare, shows upon, a silent stare.

Knowing that, the sun shall rise, upon the lonely, broken
Skies, for the night, no longer here, has departed within
The fear. For I know, that night shall come, as I look, and
Wonder why, my soul now binds, to see the light.

GERALD A. GOTT
September 27, 2005

SILENT SOUNDS

Sounds which linger, just beyond
The hollow log, which lie beneath,
The old oak tree.

Sounds of beauty, of golden harps,
Which bring the peace, to all the hearts,
Find the melodies, of years gone by, to
Find the tears, far inside.

The soul which breaks, and opens bare,
For all to see, for all to share. Only
Joy within the tune, brings the sunlight,
To shine on you.

Radiant light within your eyes, for your
Soul, comes from the night, finding solace,
With such delight.

Silent sounds within the green, no one hears,
But only me, for the sorrow, which lies beneath,
The broken soul, no one can see.

GERALD A. GOTT
29 October 2013

HUMAN VOICES

How long is time, I wonder why, and yet
I hear, no sound nor cry. I crave to hear,
But just one voice, and yet I know, that is my
Choice.

To hear a whisper, within my ear, the joy of
Sound, is very near, which brings about a
Silent tear. Joy at last fills my soul, for I am
Alive, and not alone.

Human voices so dear to me, have come again.
To waken me, to let me know, that time has passed,
That dreaded fear, has gone at last.

The fear of silence, forever more, to last forever,
Upon the shores, for sound alone, within the ear, can
Change the soul, of silent fear.

GERALD A. GOTT
30 October 2013

WHISPERING WINDS

Ever so silent, air flowing with rustling winds,
As silent clouds move within the heavens. For
Only time, which never fails, follow the winds,
Upon their sail.

Searching the heavens, within the sphere, knowing
Full well, the skies are clear. Clear of worry, sorrow,
And pain. Silently they release their rain.

Nourishment for earth below, for life itself begins to
Flow, showing signs of healthy birth, beginning of
Time, upon this earth.

Blooms of flowers, which do array, O' how they
Brighten the earth, this silent day. Colors of wonder,
Befuddle the mind, for beauty itself, has captured
The time.

Whispering winds which silently stalk, the heavens
Of blue, which never have moved, due to their beauty,
Of shimmering hue.

GERALD A. GOTT
17 November 2013

DAYS OF SOLACE

Solace surrounds my very being, ever
So gently, softly in sound, touching my
Heart strings, which play like the clown.

The tears which flow, as rivers from creeks,
Reaching for earth, as they fall, from my cheeks.
Upon the flowers, and grass, freshness anew, brings
New life, with a vibrant hue.

Only in death, is beauty the strength, which
Holds the fiber, within the soul, for only
Man knows.

This day, will never be changed, as other
Days, are always the same. Solace from
Others, I never have met, and yet it is with
Kindness, I ever have shed.

As darkness now falls, and day light, now
Gone, alone with my solace, is all that I have,
Seeking for someone, to give me their hand.

GERALD A. GOTT
27 December 2013

QUIET MOMENTS

How refreshing is the sound, the blissful melodies
Which surround, the time of day, beneath the clouds.
Only nature can you hear, for within there is no fear.

Peace abounds throughout the sphere, tunes of beauty,
For all to hear. For this moment, all alone, finds the
Heaven's only tone.

Seeking out the sounds to hear, for all around me,
Within the sphere, lies the beauty, so very near. If life
Alone were just so dear, all of nature, would sound
So clear.

Alas my time, has quickly vanished, leaving beauty, where
Man was banished, for the silent sounds, so clear, always
There, always near.

GERALD A. GOTT
1 January 2014

DEPRESSION

From the blue, when all is well, approaching
Darkness appears, damping the very soul, which
Lies in wait.

Surrounding the realm, which is ever present, taking
All away, peace of mind, joyful soul, gleaming eyes of
Delight. Only darkness prevails, with no hope in sight,
For in the fog, lies the solemn, pain and fright.

Alone in solitude, no peace of mind, for the darken
Halls, are hid from sight. The halls within our very
Mind, find no peace, for this our plight.

Our very soul, torn apart, never mending, forever
Waiting, for one ray of light, blissful days and searching
Souls, finding peace forever known.

GERALD A. GOTT
8 January 2014

FRIENDS

Time has left me all alone, the
Friends I laughed with, no longer
Here, time has taken, those so close
And near.

In times of sorrow, my friends, were
There, as if tomorrow, was yesterday,
I find myself, longing for those days, within
The stillness, you can hear, their silent voices,
With gladness cheer, you're not alone, for
We are here.

As darkness appears, just above the sun, I stop
And wonder, when is my time, my time to run.
Seeking friendship's no longer here, longing for
Those, I held so dear.

Another day, has come and gone, as I look, into
The sun, as if tomorrow, will never come. For
Time has taken, those I love, forever gone, beyond
The sun.

GERALD A. GOTT
29 August 2014

LASTING FRIENDSHIP

To have a friend, in ending years, is like the
tear drops upon the pond, as the circle expands
its depth, the drop ensures, the time we met.

Your 83, between the trees, and often wonder,
when did we meet. O' the times, we sat and laughed,
until our sides hurt, and laughed some more.

Now time has taken, your strength away, I take your
hand, another day, to say hello, to a friend of many
years, holding back, the hidden tears.

Knowing well, this could be the last time, our eyes
will meet, seeking laughter, one more time, for bones
are old, and muscles weak, only time is what we seek.
You're my friend, until the end, and always will be, as
time began.

What an honor, to call you friend, for the years, have passed
us by, and only time, has time to cry. For as we grow old,
and look around, we find our friends, cannot be found.

Gerald A. Gott
12/31/2016

Nature

RAIN DROPS

As the cold wind blows, and raindrops
Fall, as if their snow, upon the ground, of
No return, I wonder if, this world will learn,
The pain and blood, which have been shed, and
Never wish the two were wed.

As the puddles form their own beginning, I
Often think, which one is winning. The wind
Which blows, upon the plains, or will it be the
Lasting rain.

The cold, which pierces the very soul, brings
Forth the truth, for all to know. My life today,
Shall not return, nor my soul, will ever burn.

I see and feel the warmth aside, and know that
Bitter cold inside. What seems as warmth, is
Death at hand, standing, waiting, just for man.

For in the cold of death itself, no soul shall
Feel, the bitterness, for death has claimed an
Empty shell.

GERALD A. GOTT
21 December 1995

MOUNTAIN TOP

Above the trees, so out of view,
Within the skies, that cannot hide,
To hear the quietness, and know you're
Near, for on the mountain top, there is
No fear.

Tree tops appear as sphere's, silently watching,
Waiting, for the clouds, to come near. Reaching
Out to touch, the vapor's within reach, only to
Find emptiness, and solitude, have come too soon.

Rocks adore the cliffs, which hang like solemn giants,
Protecting every inch in sight, for they, are the lone,
Stringent knights.

Rivers which caress, the new born grass, which supplies
Ample nourishment, for fish and fowl alike, waters which
Flow, and never die.

Life itself upon the top, where skies reach out, and tree
Top's shout, silently the watch goes on, upon the river's,
Silent roar, high above, the eagle's soar.

GERALD A. GOTT
29 January 1996

RUSTLE AMONG THE TREES

Lonely as I stand, and wonder where this
Life began. I'm above the lower greens,
I often float, among the trees.

Endless drifts, of current streams, the shade of
Color, appears to dream. All about the boundless
Skies, I hear a whisper, and then a cry.

Why alone, within the skies, for all the world beneath
My soul, among the leaves, with foliage near, the cries
Come out, why all the fear!

Consumed by all, and yet alone, experience tells us,
Within ourselves, we live for life, for in our souls, is
Where we hide.

The beauty of the evergreens, is like a ship, upon the
Seas, always present, never near, it's like the stars, and
Lonely years.

GERALD A. GOTT
13 April 1996

IN THE SHADOWS

Beneath the glimmering leaves of green,
I look upon the valley, of autumn leaves,
Covered deep, as waves upon the open
Sea.

My soul embraces thy beauty, which I cannot
Touch, the searing pain, of love lost now, for
In the meadows, my heart in silence, frowns.

Thy lonely tear, falls for eternity, the wound
Inside, shall never heal, my broken heart, I
Fall and kneel.

Never more to touch your soul, for in the
Meadows, is where you go, to dance and
Sing, and always smile, for I shall come,
Within a mile.

I stand within the shade of light, for I am here,
Throughout the night. You shall never, have
To fear, for I am always near.

In the shadows, I stand alone, as the guard, of
One's own soul, no harm shall come, to thee this
Night, for my shield's, the lonesome might.

GERALD A. GOTT
27 April 1996

SUN RISE

As morning breaks, the
Dew drops sway, silent in the wind,
The rays of heaven, appear just beyond
The rim.

How beautiful the light appears to be, as
Rays upon the ground, brings life forth,
Reaching for the skies, upon the rays, of heaven's
Light.

The gold, mixed with crescent orange, becomes red against
The blue, for all the world, to cast its
Eye, upon the beauty, of the sky.

As pillars reach to heaven's gate, endless clouds
Of no return, surround the throne, and God's own Son.

No artist could ever paint the beauty, in heaven's
Gate, for only He, from which it comes, had years ago,
Said, "it is done."

GERALD A. GOTT
16 July 1996

SILENT GREENS

Autumn comes, amid the changing of
The colors, bright yellows, red, and orange,
With a shade of brown, and green.

Silently they change, with no sound, for all
The world, shall see, the changing of the guard.
Meadows bow, in reverence to the sky, for all
Around, their beauty cannot hide.

Limbs as old, as granite mixed, between the rocks,
Standing still through breezes, rain, and fog, only
Time itself, will only know, the beauty of the guard,
For in the mid, of seasons change, the old limbs stand,
In silent rain.

Silent greens kept by God, for only man, has
Spoiled the sod, broken branches, sawed off limbs,
Leaves of beauty, left by man.

Silently, they stand their watch, these limbs of old,
Full of beauty, to unfold. In the heaven's, a voice is
Heard, change the colors, upon the earth.

GERALD A. GOTT
27 July 1996

BREAKING WATER

The sound of breaking waves, upon the
Rocks, of no decay, for endless years, the
Same old sound, upon the waves, striking
Ground.

Above on high, the sounds of life, for in the
Heaven's, within the skies, the sounds continue,
The endless cries.

Below the deep, of blue green surf, there is another,
Which does not thirst, for in the depths, of deep blue
Seas, there lies a quietness, which is serene.

As the sound, leaves ocean floors, to rush upon, like
Open doors, to meet its end, and then return, upon
The tide, of constant death, as they break, we hold
Our breath.

The sprays which shatter, within the skies, disappear
And seek to hide, no more to rush, like open doors, for
All the mist, upon the floor.

GERALD A. GOTT
28 July 1996

169

DEATH OF A FLOWER

Early in the misty morning, thy stems reach for
Just a drop of dew, seeking life from heavens doors.
Ever so slightly, gentle are the drops, which fall upon
Thy dry and parched fibers, giving life once more.

As the wetness surrounds thee, life which was dead, now
Finds strength, upward, ever so upward, reaching for the
Skies, where only silence, and beauty, can abide.

The morning sun, warms and hastens inward growth, for
Life belongs to Him, who starts and melts the snow. The
Crown, which adorns the lonely stem, adds color, and beauty,
Which man alone, can stand.

The fragrance, which delights, the senses of the mind, are held
Captive, by this shining crown, the beauty, and the fragrance,
So little time they have, for in the time of noon day, their beauty
Shall have passed.

The beauty of the crown, no longer stands abreast, for in the time
Of seasons, the crown, has met its death.

GERALD A. GOTT
1 August 1996

RIPPLES IN THE WATER

Silently waiting, smooth as glass, no
One breathing, all seemed glad, for the
Day, had come at last.

Waters standing, no one near, for the
Souls, have fled in fear. Waiting till
Time itself, has fled away, for the waters
Shall move today.

As the heaven's open wide, receives a
Soul, which seems to glide, within the
Waters, deep inside.

Ripples form, which run away, happy for
This blessed day,for the soul, has seen the
Light, as the ripples, disappear from sight.

Standing, waiting, silently alone, for there
Are no ripples, to be shown, grief has stricken,
Water's deep, as no soul, came forth to weep.

How long shall waters, silent watch, transfixed
In time, will count the cost, for souls without, the
Ripples touch, shall miss the blessing, which cost
So much.

GERALD A. GOTT
18 March 1997

WOLVES

Within the mist, which blinds the eye, there
Comes a sound, a distant cry.
For only sounds, of great despair, fall upon,
Those silent ears.

Silent trees, of ageless time, stand alone,
And hear their cry.
Whispers now, and ever more, are heard
Throughout, the timbers core.

Softely as, the leaves which fall, came the sound,
Which all men call.
Death itself, can hear their cry,
For the sound, is clear tonight.

Upon the paws, of gentle sway, lies the breath,
You heard today.
Glaring forth, through timbers way, came
Their cry, with much dismay.
Silently they watch their prey, lurking just,
Beyond the grave.

GERALD A. GOTT
Before 8 February 1999

AMBERS OF SUN LIGHT

Rays of life, which filter through, clouds
Of darkness, life anew, within seamless skies,
Which never die.

Warm ambers, which heat the soul, upon the
Hill, which did not show, pain and suffering, of
King and might, for the sun, had turned to night.

Eyes upon heaven's gate, for only darkness, did
Escape. Upon the world, of sin and shame, died
The King, who came to claim.

For all He wanted, was to save the souls, of them
Who cried, with hate below, to curse His name, when
Time began.

For all the fear, which man has felt, was due because,
Their knees weren't knelt, before the King, which died they
Say, to rise again, another day. For the King, alive and well,
Defeated death, upon that hill.

For He alone, has loved us all, there are a few, who heard
His call, upon their broken souls, His hand did lay, for these
Alone, shall rise again, to see their Lord, another day.

GERALD A. GOTT
19 February 2000

173

LITTLE FLOWER

Little flower in the breeze, how I love thy
Simple sway, in the sunlight of early day,
Came the smile, of God this way. With
Pleasant colors of array, I search the fields,
For gleaming lights, of little crystals, of
Delight. Within the blossom,the eye can see,
The mighty love, of God for thee. For the
Pedals, spaced within your frame, show the
Love and not the shame. For God alone, with
Love in hand, created all, about the land.
Within the sight, of human eyes came the day
Which turned to night.

For the seasons, passed us by, but thy beauty,
Caught the eye, within the flower, of silent
Might, lies the story, for this I cry.

For God alone, allowed this day, for me to
See, thy beauty's sway. Upon the dormant,
Flower's bed, lies the crystal, tears I shed.
For the Lord, and He alone, has taken thee,
Away to home.

GERALD A. GOTT
2001

DISTANCE

So close and yet not near, for love itself,
Has fled in fear. For the lashing of the wind,
Has torn the chimes, so deep within.

Gone are drops, of dew not new, for all the
Love, I had for you, within the realm, of flesh
And bone. In constant pain, is where I roam, to
Speak is like, the distant skies, so far away, which
Blurs' the eye.

Yearning like a new born dove, finding flight, away
From love. Seeking distance within the void, finding
Nothing, but the soiled, littered memories of the past,
Seeking love, which did not last.

Alone in death, ever silent into the night, for in the
Darkness, where there's no light, I seek the love, within the
Wind, to find it's gone, beyond the rim.

GERALD A. GOTT
28 April 2001

EYES OF STEEL

Silently blue eyes', watch under the moons',
Dim light, surveying the land, searching for a
Sign of life.

Eyes of coal bolt blue, ear's which hear its'
Prey, within the depths, of endless cries, this
Creature crept.

In the stillness, of the meadows, movement seen by
Pools of blue, flare open wide, for its' prey, is now in sight.

Muscles tense, like bands of steel, lunging forward
To make the kill, finding blood, a drop away, holding
Fast, another day.

For the fangs, sharp as steel, has struck its prey, in
Sudden pain. His prey has lost, the flight for life, for yet
Another will feed tonight.

Now the creature, with bloody teeth, feeds the rest, which are
Beneath. Cries from pups, no longer hungry, feed upon the
Lifeless for, just before the winter storm.

GERALD A. GOTT
21 August 2001

HEAVENLY WATERS

Dampness which, softens' the ground beneath,
Like living water, where life abodes, brings
Freshness to the soul.

Upon the beauty, of the land, where God, has
Laid His hand. Springs forth life, where none
Exist, for God Himself, within the mist.

Lightly falling, like angels from the sky, dew drops
Touching, bringing life, where life did hide. Heaven
Above in endless blue, skies of glory, of beauty untold,
Shall at last, for man unfold.

O' the freshness, the scent of life, for within my soul,
Which seeks' new life, I cleave upon, the dew drops new,
Savoring scent's, of life itself, upon my soul, the dew
Which melts.
Soften O', the harden ground, for life anew, shall
Abound, bringing forth, the rays of life, for now
I know, for who He died.

GERALD A. GOTT
1 March 2002

SOUNDS OF CREATION

Hear the rushing sea's, upon heaven's gates, with
Gentle swaying, of cloud's now past. The bird's which
Sing, with melodies of joy, cluster around the fearless skies.

Tree's of amber, of strength and age, stand before the timeless
Gate, for all to see, within their time, and never wonder, for in their
Mind, lies their beauty, for all mankind.

Ocean's floor, beneath the moon, rest the cold, and silent form, eye's
So darken, within the night, only God, knows of its' might. Than the
Beauty, of the day, came along with gentle sway.

Heaven thunders overhead, as the snowflakes, make their bed, upon
The soft and dew soaked ground, there are no two, which can be found.

God above, with glories might, with gentle hands, and loving heart,
Started life, which now is short. Because of man, and man alone, life
Is gone, and not atoned.

GERALD A. GOTT
24 July 2002

BEFORE DAWN

Early in the morning, just before the sun,
Peaks over the hills, I search the heaven's
For just a glimpse, of thy glory.

As the light, appears upon the land, the
Array of colors, blind the eye's which, so
Diligently seek thee.

The hue's of blue, from heaven's gate, upon
The green's, mixed with amber gold, which
Warms the soul. Water's gently flowing, like
Melodies of blissful music, soothing body and
Soul alike.

Feathered friends in branches tall, while on the
Ground the creatures craw, with heaven's eye,
Upon them all.

The glory I see, around me stands, for all of this,
Was done for man, for God alone, within the sky,
Is ever watching, with loving eyes.

GERALD A. GOTT
15 July 2002

SPARROW'S FLIGHT

As if by day, or by night, wonders of
The sparrow's flight. Within the clouds,
For fear of sight, the sparrow flies,
Throughout the night.

I search the skies, for feathered friends,
Looking for, the slightest glimpse, so as to
Know, my heart's content

Only wings of feathers shown, will I ever
Begin to know, why did God create thee
Soft? To touch thy feathers, would cleanse
My heart.

I know within, my soul's delight, today's the
Day, you're within my sight. O' what joy, the
Heaven's make, for the gentle hand, of God's
Own love, touched my feathered, friend above.

GERALD A. GOTT
7 February 2006

FLOWERS ADRIFT

Little flowers drifting by, having fun
Beneath the skies, for the tears in the
Past, have left thy gleaming eyes at
Last.

Happy are the days ahead, laughter, giggling,
Having fun, running, hiding beneath the sun. For
All the cares of yesterday, left behind in
Disarray, looking just ahead, where joy abides,
Knowing fear has no place to hide.

Only joy of new day found, surrounds the
Flowers upon the ground. Healthy, happy,
Little flower's, only beauty is thy crown.

Rest my little ones now gone, sleep anew,
For in the song, are the whispers, forever
Gone. Children are the flowers, upon the
Ground, only laughter is their song.

GERALD A. GOTT
23 January 2014

WINTERY WIND

Winds howling through the air, for no
One, appears to care, for lighter snow,
Has fallen upon the souls, which seemed
Unmoved, within the cold.

Like crystals within the wind, they cover
Land, just like the sand. Clinging to the life
Below, covered with a dust of snow. Beauty
Beyond belief, only one shall watch and see.

Pure as pearls beneath the sea, upon the land,
For all to greet, white and clean, like daybreak
New, for all to feel, except a few.

Only time will expel, all the beauty, which has
Fell, leaving darkness upon the ground, which
The crystal's fallen found.

GERALD A. GOTT
25 January 2014

HILLS OF BEAUTY

O' the beauty of thy strength, for
Beside thee, stands the link, which
Draws your might, before the sun,
For the children begin to run.

How they play, with joy delight, beaming
Brightness within our sight. For the
Hills of trees asunder, draw the mind,
With gazing wonder.

As the trees, with snowflakes resting,
Appear as stars, within the night, beauty
Resting within our sight, with decorations
Of green and white.

For when they lose, their coat of snow,
Beauty rises from below, for all to see,
With hearts aglow.

GERALD A. GOTT
8 February 2014

COLD WINDS

The sting of piercing ice, flowing like
Rivers, with no direction in sight, for
Cold alone, will take the ones, for which
It holds.

Life lingers as if dead, yet in time, shall
Strive to seek it's life, when warmth once
Again, shall move life within, seeking the
Life of breath, far beneath.

The winds are howling, as wolves seeking
Death, of air which vapor's show, the life
Within the frozen souls. Ever lurking beneath,
The frozen snow.

Stillness wait's, in silent bliss, for the souls,
The cold has missed, ever looking for another,
For the pups, now seek their mother.

For the warmth, within the cold, protects
The pups from winter's soul, until the time,
The sun will shine. For the snow, shall melt
Away, for the pups, to run and play.

GERALD A. GOTT
28 February 2014

SUNLIGHT

O' the beauty, of rays of light, which
Breakthrough, the thicken hue, brightness
Abounds, with life anew, vibrant colors
Now adore, earth's lush colors, to the core.

To touch the colors, with ones on hand, the
Beauty, which command's, the awe of man. For
In time, the beauty fades, replaced by yet,
Another wonder of stormy nights.

Purity itself, touching the earth, ever so gentle,
And yet so rigid, cold to the touch, with waves of
White powder, falling down from heaven's paint
Brush. Every snow flake, different in beauty, size
And shape.

For all of the wonder's, from God's own hand, are
To remind us all, we are only men. As the flower's,
Cover the land, we will soon, return to sand. Do
Not cry, for beauty's sake, for no tears, shall
Ever fall, upon the heaven's, golden gates.

GERALD A. GOTT
4 June 2014

FEATHERED FRIENDS

How majestic in the sky, are your
Movements, which can't deny, thy
Strength and skill, before the night.

Lovely are thy darting eyes, ever
Searching from the skies, seeking
Movement from below, soaring down
As lightning strikes, swiftly as the
Bird in flight.

As you sit, upon the branch, pruning
Feather's, so they will match, making
Ready to fly away, seeking freedom,
Another day.

O' the beauty, which God has given,
Releases joy, upon the land, as you
Fly, within our sight, landing just
Before the night.

GERALD A. GOTT
1 August 2014

SNOWFLAKE

Softly as the wind, beauty alone
Appears within, crystal ice which
Meets the eye, for some reason,
Brings joy inside.

White flakes, for all to see, cover
The land, as if by sea, all different,
To the eye, for their beauty, shall
Shortly die.

Winter wind, which brings the cold,
Holds the crystal's, which now unfold,
Diamond's upon the land, which forever
Will always stand.

Alone and sleek, on mountain top's, sight's
Beyond, the mind of man, for God alone, with
Grace and might, created all by gentle hands.

GERALD A. GOTT
16 December 2014

MAJESTIC SEAS

How the depths, have kept thy hue,
Far within the coral blue, silent sea's
Of beauty rest, hidden treasure's in
Pirate's chest, guarded by the fear
Of death.

O' the wonder's, found below, beauty
Lie's in covered cove's, creature's roam
The sea's beneath, where the eyes, of
Man can't see.

Glistening from the moon light skies,
Hear the wave's, as they cry, seeking
Solace, from beneath, as the wave's, rush
For shore, for this alone, will be no more.

Casting beauty, of crystal's light, softly
Sounding, beauty's plight, along their
Travels, through the night. For in time,
When this began, upon the shore's, in crystal
Sand.

GERALD A. GOTT
13 February 2015

WITHIN THE CLOUDS

Transparent to the eyes
Below, ever searching, for
This I know, wonders from the
Distant gates, just beyond, our
Blinded gaze.

Deep within the hidden blue, forms
Which search, outside the hue, seeking
Substance of no return, for in the heat,
They all but burned.

Eyes below, searching depths, in the
Distance, beyond man's reach, is the
Glory, and blessed peace. Eternal time
Shall never pass, for we have reached,
Our home at last.

GERALD A. GOTT
19 March 2015

Darkness, Sins, and Evil

ONLY DARKNESS

I look at darkness as if it were day,
To embrace its coldness, and seek the
Solitude of never ending silence.

For time itself shall run its course,
But the darkness which seems like day
Shall always be, it consumes me like
The sun embraces the skies.

I loathe the day, the brightness of
The skies, for in them, there is the lie.
For what is the lie, that man cannot see,
Only in darkness, shall it be, the time
For what it really is, nothing but a timeless pit.

I seek the darkness, for there in, there is
A void, a cavern of no return, only darkness
Understand the emptiness within me.

No one knows the hell I see,
No one knows the darkness I seek,
My day is near and darkness waits,
For in darkness, there is no day.

The souls which cried within the day,
Shall no longer be heard in darkness
I pray.

For even the wind, is silent, in awe,
In utter serenity. For in darkness
So vast and wide, you can't hear the
Voices of those who died.

I see the beauty of daylight near,
For only in darkness, I hide my fear.

GERALD A. GOTT
30 December 1994

LONELY DEPTHS

The blackness engulfs my very soul,
I am not alive, as I see nothing, and
Yet I know.

I move, and feel only emptiness,
I grasp at air and the mist, which
Surrounds me.

The heat I feel is beyond belief,
And yet there is no one here, it
Seems, but me.

I sense within these dark lonely depths,
Which swallow me up as a great cavern,
The souls of them who are in torment, and
Pain, shall I ever see, another living
Soul again?

I bit my tongue, for the pain is great,
For I know now, I am among the dead. I
Wish no man upon this place.

My fear, exceeds the boundaries of my
Soul, I cannot turn away, for death and
Hell are everywhere.

I cry, can no one hear, has God
Forsaken me? For this I fear!

GERALD A. GOTT
10 January 1995

ASYLUM

The sounds which are about me, I cannot
Stand, for in their spirit, a wickedness seethes,
For they are around me, as sharks in the sea.

The scent of blood, fills their nostrils, as
Water fills the brook, my heart feels faint, my
Soul trembles within, for all this evil, I cannot
Think.

I was safe inside, for this I thought, but now I
Know, it was for naught. The joy which was,
And is no more, my spirit's grieved, for this
They know, and surely see.

I cry within this frame of mine, O Lord, my God,
Why can't I find, the peace of heart, which once
Was mine. For all the love, I have for thee, I beg
Forgive them, for this I plea.

They scream as those, in days of old, for they know
Not, the sin they're in, nor the fear, that's crept in, for
The pews are full of souls, shouting, screaming, shaking
Heads, they know not, their souls are dead.

Dead to sin, which has crept in, for their minds are full of
Hate, and yet they cheer, for another day. As this lonely
Figure leaves, broken hearted, knowing well, all has passed,
With Satan's spell.

Heart's are broken, spirits crushed, as the crowd leaves in
A rush, silent walls which heard them all, stand alone in darken
Halls. For the man, which loved them so, shuts the doors, upon
The cold, for within his broken heart, the figure stands, and then
Departs

GERALD A. GOTT
30 November 1995

193

PENITENCE

Have I not asked, and not received, the soul
And spirit, which has passed, life is blind, in
Turbulent times, for this my cause, is surely mine.

I seek the light, and find the night, which
Bounds my soul, for that's unknown. My soul
Is dampened, my spirit's gone, for within my
Eyes, there is no song.

Only blindness within my reach, for my eyes, they
Cannot see. The beauty which is, and yet not
Near, I cannot see, for all my fear.

Dismay surrounds me, with little hope,
The grief I bear, is like a yoke, about my
Neck, nowhere to go.

Only I, can see the realm, for in the depths,
Of soundless souls, I hear their cries, where
Shall they go?

GERALD A. GOTT
25 December 1995

LOATHE

From within the darken cells, of
Life itself, no one shall tell, of the
Darkness, which lies within, for the
Soul weeps, and cannot win.

From within the eyes themselves, only
Blackness lives and dwells. Seeing silent
Souls about, wandering aimlessly from without.

From within the ears, so near, the cries, of
Those who can't be reached, for all the love, and
Softness preached.

From within the soul, so vast, lies the open sore
At last. Swollen from the sin within, causing death,
To man again.

From the darken cells of life, only death will never
Hide, for death shall always, seek for one, for the soul,
Shall not return.

GERALD A. GOTT
3 January 1996

FLAMES

In the darken depths of blue, I hear the souls,
Which cannot move, with the green mist, which
Prevails, for all these screams, are down in hell.

Darken paths of no return, for the flames, shall
Always burn, flesh upon the open flames, for the
Souls, will never gain, as they cry out, with endless pain.

Thirst upon the desert sands, for I cannot see my
Hands, just a drop of moisture please, for my tongue,
In cheek, does cleave.

In the darken, depths of hell, no one knows, or ever
Will, why the souls, in dire distress, seek to find the
Hope of bliss.

Reaching out within the pit, for a drop of something
Wet, only sadness meets their dreams, as they wake,
And hear their screams.

GERALD A. GOTT
20 March 1996

UNWORTHY

As dirt covers the ground, the sins of
Man, will abound, no good is man, because
Of sin, their souls shall wrestle, and never win.

Unworthy to love, and yet still is, the
Soul of man, shall always live. No Soul
Can hide, from thee, O' God, the souls of
Man, before thy eyes.

As the currents, form and run, beneath the sea's,
The sin of man, will always be, as sands upon the
Open beach.

Denied the heaven's, as they are, the sin, as yet, has
Kept them marred. For sin alone, has sliced their souls,
From the portals, of joys unknown.

As the dirt, upon the ground, they shall not see, nor hear
The sound, of Angels singing, within the clouds. For sin
Has taken, their part away, from their God, and open gates.

GERALD A. GOTT
21 March 1996

THE EMPTY SILL

Upon the sill, from where I watch,
Into the night, there lies the fight, for
Hell has come, in fury and wrath, upon
The sill, there comes a draft.

In the darkness, of the night, one can hear,
The screams and fright, only day break, can
Peace abide.

In my mind, and in my soul, I pray for silence,
To unfold. It was the graveyard, and its sights,
For which I gazed, throughout the night.

I awake, and trimmer, with fear inside, for I
Thought, I surely died. Upon the graveyard, of
Dirt and bones, my place is there, for this I know.

My body's numb, and cold to feel, just look for me,
Upon the sill. My soul is free, just like the wind, upon
The sill, where there's no sin.

GERALD A. GOTT
25 June 1996

DARKEN WALLS

Down the slippery, slimy sides, I
Find that darkness, is all that hides,
The death within, the darken hell, is
Where the souls, have surely fell.

Within the reach, of no man's hands, only
Darken souls can stand, the light of day,
Which does not shine, because of darkness,
Man is blind.

Fear which grasp, the desperate souls, which call and cry,
For no one's near, for in the darken walls of death,
Souls which seek, for one to hear, can only wait,
Amongst the fear.

Succumb, by darken walls of hate, the souls now wander,
Searching lonely empty walls, I can hear, the souls now call,
Come to me, O' soul of night, for now's the time, for us to cry.

With much despair, the souls depart, for utter silence, waits in
The dark. To start again, the pain which fell, from the walls, of death, and
Hell.

GERALD A. GOTT
10 September 1996

SPHERE OF DARKNESS

Darkness which prevails, where the eye,
Has often failed, as solitude entombs, like the
Wind, which always moves.

Forbidding darkness, which holds the
Souls, only touched, by those of stone.

Darkness shadows every move, reaching out,
With darken doom. Upon the sorrows,
Of souls now lost, into the pit,
Where there's no law.

Light which warms, the darken souls, cannot reach,
The inner folds, stands without, the darken sphere,
For inside, is only fear.

Melodies of tunes unheard, try and break, the silent
Curse, only darkness which prevails, claims the soul's,
Eternal hell.

GERALD A. GOTT
7 January 1997

DARKEN SOUL

Darken soul of deceit, how often, we
Seem to meet. How I fight thee, with all
My strength, and yet, the battle, you often see.

Within the depths, of no return, my darken soul, for
Freedom yearns. In blackness, pitched in empty eyes,
I hear the souls, their silent cries.

Crying out, in anguish pain, never more, to feel the rain.
For in the darkness, no soul is sane, only bleakness, and
Fear remain.

Bound by time, which never ends, reaching forward, towards
The winds, darken souls, in anguish pain, death itself, has locked
In chains.

Tombs of death, this soul has met, far in the darken, caves which
Shed, blacken Erie moonless spots, for in these tombs, the souls
Which rot, will never see, nor hear the sound, of life itself, above
The ground.

GERALD A. GOTT
9 July 1997

INNER DARKNESS

The light that's bright within my sight,
Becomes a cloud, of darken might, which
Overtakes the soul, as if it's night.

The strength in which it moves the soul, into
Oblivion of despair, for no one ever seems to
Care. O' darken soul in darkness light, the cry
Of death, is heard tonight.

For in the grasp of death and pain, my soul does
Watch, as if the rain, could wash away the sorrows
Near, in death my soul, no longer fears.

O' bright and sunny skies, for within this shell of mine,
I hide the sorrows of today, to keep within the darken
Walls, for there is no one, to hear my call.

GERALD A. GOTT
10 October 2001

DARKENED MIST

Upon the light, appears the gray, the morning dust,
Upon the clay. Shadows darken morning skies, for
Only darkness, blinds the eye.

With each breath, drawn within its depth, darken
Memories drown the light, for in darkness, hides the
Fright. Darkness rules the very thought, of the light,
With morning dust, upon the clay, appears like rust.

Only darkness remains, no one sees, only in
Darkness, can evil breed. Evil which man should
Fear, and dread. Reaching forth to embrace, upon the
Human race.

Consumed within body and soul, darken eyes, now seem
To glow, for the time, shall come to all, how did darkness,
Find my soul. Within the slippery, darken void, upon my
Chest, my heart did beat, to the drum, of defeat.

Creeping slowly, evermore, silent darkness evil's core,
Within my soul, the darken doors, opened once, upon the
Cords. Early darkness, upon the light, appears as gray,
Against the night.

GERALD A. GOTT
7 July 2006

DARKNESS FOLLOWS

In the mist of no return, lingers fear
So very near, closing in and yet not
Clear, ever closer darken veil, coming
From the pit of hell.

Fear surrounds the fields of blue, gleaming
Brightness from its hue. Killing hope with
Great despair, leaving no one, who is aware,
Darkness follows everywhere.

Running to the light ahead, ever closer,
Within a step, never knowing when the fear,
Grasping heart, with little air. For only
Darkness now abides, for no one, heard my cry.

In the depths of no return, only bleak and
Lonely forms, roam the cold and darken halls,
For there is none, to hear their calls. Ever more
Shall darkness bind, for in the shadows, is where
It hides.

GERALD A. GOTT
24 January 2014

A TIME TO WEEP

In times of sadness, and of grief, there are
The tears, which hide beneath, flowing from
The heart below, for all the world, to see
And hold.

Silent vigil with broken hearts, for our loved
One, with open eyes, did depart. Leaving only
Living tears, which flow from hearts, who loved
Them dear.

O' the day, is living long, for our hearts, have
Not the song, of happy times, so close and yet
Not near, for only silence, leaves us fear.

Daybreak and another day, sun so high, with
Brilliant light, for now it's time, to say good
By, for our hearts, have cleared our minds, for
We shall remember, in lasting time.

All the laughter and happy times, and yet in
Sadness, we must strive, to carry on, to live
Our lives. For in the future, will be our time.

GERALD A. GOTT
2 February 2014

MERCY

As I look into the sky, I said
O' Lord, why must it be I, alone,
Afraid to see, yet another day.

Darken rivers, which flow down
Stream, always moving, which can't
Be seen. Living waters, full of life,
Yet are hidden, from mans own eyes.

My soul is torn, in pieces lie, blinded
Eyes, left in darkness, never seeing,
The empty land, the light before me,
With reaching hand.

Mercy stands before my eyes, never seeing
Beneath the sky, never knowing, he heard
My cry.

For mercy holds, the keys of death, alone
I stand, with silent breath, waiting for the
Light itself, to claim my soul, from earth's
Dark hold.

GERALD A. GOTT
15 March 2014

SILENT SKIES

The wonder of the earth, so silent
Within the universe, ever so green, and
Yet with blue seas, their beauty so
Bright, filled with life.

How small man, appears to be, and yet
Have domain, over the seas. Within the
Realm, of life itself, all is needed, for
Breath alone, indeed created.

In the beauty, in darken shadows, lies
The evil, which longs to shatter, life
Itself, which doesn't matter. How short
O' man, thy life ends, how we forget, where
It began.

Thy breath alone, within the air, keeps thy
Heart, from harm and fear, and yet thy eyes,
See all there is, within thy heart, is sudden
Fear. Alone again, as if thy birth, came again
Upon this earth.

Into the blue, in silent depths, stillness lies,
Which can't be kept, sinking down, in miry clay,
For life itself, another day.

GERALD GOTT
2 April 2014

SOLEMN HOUR

Words spoken, in great despair, softly
Landing, for those who care, ripping through
The heart's now torn, due to grief for evermore.

Silence fills the crowded sphere, for all have
Come, not out of fear, but to say, goodby again,
To the one, who's left the land.

The soul has left, the body still, the love has
Gone, beyond the hills, into the everlasting
Skies, for now it's time, to say goodby.

Broken heart's and soul's now crushed, moving
As, if there's no rush, hunger gone, and tear's
Still wet, for in time, some will forget. For all
The soul's, which now have met, this lonely
Hour of regret.

GERALD A. GOTT
1 August 2014

SHADOW OF EVIL

Within the dampen, cloud of darkness,
Lies the evil, lurking just beyond the
Light. No sound is heard, no eye can see,
.   The evil waiting, for soul's in need.

Always there, for just one chance, to
Strike, the soul's, with piercing lance,
To break the spirit, within man's cast.

To wonder why, the soul's so dark,
Searching light, for just one spark,
Dismal failure, before the fall, for
The evil, is here for all.

Waiting, lurking, just beyond the light,
For a moment, for a chance to strike, for
The soul's, still unknowing, continue in
The night.

Laughter reigns, above the sight, of decay
Without a cry, for the end, with much dismay,
Has settled in, for man again.

GERALD A. GOTT
22 November 2014

REAPER OF SORROW

O' the darkness, within the day, stands
In the sunlight, covered by haze. The
Curved blade now sharpen, ready to graze.

Ever so gently, grazing the soul's, standing
And watching, within the cold gray. Not
Knowing that danger, await's them this
Day.

As grains of sand, which cover the beach,
Will no longer be, for heaven to reach. As
Darkness unfolds, the reaper has come, and
Taken the soul's.

The whaling of sorrow, now heard all around,
For love has now left us, with heads hanging
Down. Broken heart's shattered, in sorrow
And grief, for it's too late, for them to believe.

GERALD A. GOTT
1 January 2015

EVIL

As the cloud of depression sets in, only
Silent darkness, consumes my soul. I often
Wonder, when the time, had passed me by, I find
Myself, asking why.

The hiding place, of nowhere man, has taken
Hold, and tied my hands. So dark that light,
Is but a glimmer, consumes the soul.

There is no hope, within the darken bowels of
Dismay, for no light shall shine upon this day.
Soul is consumed no more to see, which life could
Mean, for evil has, in anguish pain, blinded soul's
Within the rain.

Evil blinding soul's of man, as they disappear, like
Grains of sand, ever searching, wondering why, for
In the darkness, souls languish, while seeking light.
Never seeing before their eye's, the hope they have,
Before they die.

GERALD A. GOTT
19 August 2015

Death and the Grave

LONELY TOMBSTONE

As I lay here day and night
I know the souls who are in sight,
For I can't see them, for I am blind.

The silence is like death itself,
No movement within, this cell at night,
For I am confined, deep with inside.

The wind howls like the wolves on the plains,
For they are free, free from the pain,
The pain of darkness, which never ends, the
Pain of silence, which like the trees, surrounds
The skies every so bold, for this cell, so
Lonely and cold.

I know they're not far away, I can hear their
Footsteps as they fade, closer they come,
Coming this way.

They grumble as they dig another grave,
Just to fill it, at the end of the day. My
Tombstone is just above my head, you
Only get one when you are dead.

The lonely souls which surround me, are they
Who have left this day, left the world just
Above my head.

We wonder when we will see one another,
The day might come, just like thunder,
When our tombs will open and we will see,
The blinding light, which comes for me.

The ground so dark, the cold within, it
Shall not keep me, not for long, for the
Day will come, and I will be free.

I feel the worms as they crawl upon my
Rotting corpse, and yet my soul shall not

Be touched, for my soul in deep inside.

I live, and yet I am dead, I know the day
Shall come, just like the rain, when I shall
Be whole, just like the One.

GERALD A. Gott
15 January 1995

O' DEATH

O' Death, where is thy sting?
I have waited for many years,
And have not found you, anywhere.

I have wandered through the land,
Only to miss you, around the bend.
I have seen, the sorrow you bring,
Only in time to come again.

The anguish you cause, the
Deadness which holds, the living
Soul, is as dark, as your' alone.

In an instant, there is Death, never
More, to be a threat, for once you
Come, time is gone. Only sorrow and
Grief remain, in your wake, never
To behold another day.

I search the heaven's and the earth,
For no man knows, or sees your birth.
I know you're there, beyond my reach,
And one day soon, I'll feel your breach.

The day has passed and you're not here,
I look for you, and have no fear. Upon
My heart, and deep inside, I know that
You, cannot hide.

In empty winds, which float by, I
Wonder when, thou shalt die, to be
Death, no more to man,the day shall
Come, and you'll be damned.

GERALD A. GOTT
31 January 1995

CRYSTALS FROM WITHIN

My travel is far from within,
Where there is no sound, no
Light, no sin.

I am pure as the snowflakes fall,
I travel from the soul of man, to
Seek the light which binds us all.

I see the light, just beyond the eye.
This is where I must die. As I fall
Without a sound, the crystals shatter,
And fall around.

The heavens open and take them in,
No more to fall, on empty winds.

My life is but a second in time, I seek
The light, that I might have life, my time is
Short, my time is gone, upon the winds of
Time I fly, to live again, and never die.

As God is pure, so am I, for God has made
Me from inside. I am formed from within,
The only place, where there is no sin.

GERALD A. GOTT
Before 30 May 1995

OLD SOLDIER

I touched his hand, for one last time,
And in my heart, I cried, you're mine. His
Hands are cold, and all alone, there is no
Life, for none is shown.

As I look into his face, I sense a lonely, empty day.
The soul is gone, no more to be, and wonder why,
It was not me.

The flag about his coffin bears, all the pride,
For which he shared, in the uniform of old,
I bent and kissed, his face now cold.

I said within my heart that day,he shall live,
And never fade, not in time, nor memory, for
He shall always, be with me.

GERALD A. GOTT
5 October 1995

THE GRANITE'S CRY

The tombstones for which we are,
Stand in form, alone at dark, along
With other's in silent grief, for there
Is no one, here to weep.

In the silence of the night, upon the
Stones, an eerie light, shines upon the
Boulder's might, as the dew drops, slip
Down their side.

In the early morning light, I see the granite's,
As they cry, for within their mighty silent
Bounds, like a body, underground.

The soul has left, this empty shell, for the granite's
Will never tell, where or when this body fell, or if the
Soul, is down in hell.

Only darkness brings the light, whereupon the granite's
Might, appears as strength, to the eye. Only in darkness, is
When they cry.

GERALD A. GOTT
15 October 1995

MISCONCEPTION

Feel the currents as they flow, and in
Your mind, which does not know, the
Reason why you feel the hate, and
Loathe yourself another day.

As the tomb appears to wait, for my soul,
This lovely day. Into the darkness, my
Eyes do gaze, and yet I know, I'm bone and
Clay.

As my soul clings to my flesh, and in my mind,
I know I'm dead, no where to go, or ask above,
For in my heart, there is no love.

All I had, is gone away, and wonder why they had
Not stayed. I am alone with eternal clouds, as my
Body, rests underground.

GERALD A. GOTT
3 January 1996

ROCKS WHICH HIDE

Beneath the rocks, the abyss which lies, in
Its depths, the souls which hide, far within
The walls of death, the souls which wander,
And never slept.

Reaching out with cries of pain, never more to
Rest again, for in the darkness of hell itself, lies
The torments of broken wills.

As death succumbs thy very soul, and darkness
Somehow begins to show, the way to utter senseless
Pain, for thy soul, shall die again.

I cry alone, in darken cells, for there is no one, I can
Tell, of pain and grief for which I bear, for there is no
One, here to share, the darken terror, within my soul,
For only God, and Angels know.

Swept away as seamless pearls, only clouds of smoke,
Unfurl, the eyes search out, and cannot see, in the darkness,
The only meet, the endless clouds, of dark deceit.

GERALD A. GOTT
21 March 1996

THE BLUE MAZE

In the blue maze, for which I gaze, to
Feel the empty air, which surrounds me,
No life exists, but emptiness.

Peering out, from the living death which
Entombs me, the air which is filled with life,
And yet empty, are the lungs of the dead, which
Seem to inhale, emptiness.

Through the mist, from which I gaze, I see the
Sorrows of the day, for this I know, for I have seen,
Thy sorrows unfold. For in thy soul, thy body
Searches, for yet another hold.

The blue maze, O' how I hate the mist, which surrounds
Me, I breathe the air of lifeless flesh, O' how I seek a
Place of rest. No peace of mind, that I can find,within
The mist, of lifelessness.

As I drift throughout time, and yet, my body is not mine, I
Seek the rest of one's own soul, for I drift, but all alone.

GERALD A. GOTT
29 July 1996

THE REAPER

The reaper stands, with scythe in hand,
Searching through crowd's, silently moving,
No one knowing, reaching out, grabbing the
Soul, with bony hands, slithering cold.

Whisking off to darken lands, with the soul,
In his hands, never more to return, with the
Soul, now gone from man.

Into the depths, of darken bliss, you hear the
Cries, of those now missed. Into the bleakness,
Of hell itself, the soul now cast, without its shell.

The reaper peers without concern, for time awaits,
For his return, another soul, awaits his hand, to leave
The shell, of dying men.

GERALD A. GOTT
26 August 1996

DISTANT

I have been removed, no more to seek,
Nor wonder why, this cannot be, for I am
Here, but yet not whole, I search alone, for
My own soul.

To be gone, and not be found, while my body lies
Underground, only death is all around.

I walk alone this journey's end, to learn that I,
Have but one friend, and yet the distance, is clearly
Seen, for no one seems, to be with me.

The test of love, of care, and victory. I often wonder,
Why was I born, should death come early, with open arms?

GERALD A. GOTT
5 May 1996

TEARS UPON THE GRAVE

Upon the shallow ground, I find your
Soul, cannot be found, only darkness
Clouds the mind, for I have lost, what
Once was mine.

The casket silver, with golden sides, now
Holds the one, who was my bride. People
Stand, nowhere to go, seeking answers, for
Them to hold.

Never shall there be another, for God alone,
Shall see us further, as tears fall, upon your
Grave, the lonely hours, another day.

To feel your touch, and see your smile, to know
When I, first saw your eyes, I knew right then,
That you were mine.

My heart is broken, within my soul, no one to
Heal, no one to know. Alone I stand, with
Emptiness, your love I knew, and now I miss.

GERALD A. GOTT
2 December 1996

SILENT FALL

In the silent time of flight,
All the mighty, fallen cries,
Only last in time itself, for the
Curses, to be felt.

In the spiral, fallen strength, no
More greatness, on the brink, time
Has claimed, its only prize, as the
Fallen, scream and cry.

In the plunge, of no return, for the
Bottom, soon will come, like a searing,
Pain of guilt, time has come, to claim its
Wealth.

In the silent fall of man, no one seems to
Understand, time like vapor, is at hand, upon
The dying, empty land.

GERALD A. GOTT
10 January 1997

CRY OF LIFE

To touch thee, but once again, for
Life has fled, in search of silence,
Beyond the dead.

The warmth of flesh, for which there's
None, can only bring joy, of souls
Now gone.

Gleaming eyes no longer searching,
For death has closed, thy burning embers.

Sounds of laughter, no longer with us, empty
Skies, and silent tree tops, wait above the
Wilted lilies.

To Hear the breaking of the waves, and hear
The ripples as they play, amiss the rocks which
Are between, the skies and earth, which are beneath.

NO longer silent, into the night, for life has stirred, and
Is about, for life itself, shall never die, for in the twilight,
We meet the sky.

GERALD A. GOTT
5 November 1997

CRY NOT

Cry not my love, in darken woods,
Of death eternal, for time itself, has
Raised the fibers, within the crystal cells.

Hush to hear the noise, of blacken souls
About, now silence breaks, through darken
Voids, which time surrounds.

Depths of endless, chilling calls, for blacken
Souls, begin to call. Fear which last, until the
End, for fear itself, has just began.

Wish not the hour might end, darken strands
Which clutch the soul, has ended life's eternal
Goals.

Blacken as the coal of night, souls now searching,
For the light. Screaming as the fires of hell, haunt
The damned's eternal will, for the night, is like the
Sky, ever present, but denied.

Cry not my love, for I am near, to touch your soul,
When death appears. Comfort in, the hands of Light,
For thy soul, within my sight, I shall have, this very night.

GERALD A. GOTT
10 December 1997

LEGACY

As I look down from the sky, I
Sense the sorrow, within their eyes,
Fear not, loved ones far below, for
Now I'm with, the One I know.

Emerald streets of gold and pearl, only
Beauty now unfurls. No pain or sorrow,
Shall ever be, upon this body, you see at
Peace.

I stand before, my Father's throne, and find
That I'm, not here alone. Only fulfillment and
Joy abounds, for I am with my Father, with
Praise, I shout.

Dry the tears, which leave your eyes, for I am
Watching from the sky. Love each other, as I
Loved you, for in the time, which draws near,
Your souls of wonder, will meet me here.

Love, is the only word I know, my beloved one's, far below,
The King is calling, and I must go. O' the Beauty, which cannot
Stand, upon the earth, surrounds the land.

GERALD A. GOTT
4 March 1998

EVEN MOOR

Upon the watered lands, concealed by time,
Beneath the depths, where warrior's long ago,
Have slept.

Upon the battle fields, of shame and victory, where
No eye, can see their mystery. Lies the treasures, of
Ageless souls, in even moor, is where the roam.

Fallen warriors in anguish pain, plea for help, amidst the roar,
Of gallant horses, bloodied hooves, which stand above.
The dying warriors, have lost their love.

O the cry, of death we hear, upon the lands, of
Yesteryear, Forged by steel, mixed with blood, the
Souls now roam, not far above.

Lands were green, within the hills, this is where the
Souls, were killed. Loved one's searching, through
The night, in hopes of finding, their love alive.

Battles gone, upon the land, only silence, alone now
Stands. Beneath the currents, which man can't see,
There is a cry, of victory.

Through the ages, battles roar, the cry of men, upon
The shore, lifting up, as if by chance, their swords of
Honor, beside their lance.

GERALD A. GOTT
29 June 1998

DEATH

Hands of darkness, which now take hold,
Shall they have, with darken stones, of
One now gone, within the cold?

I fight the grasp, of death itself, for I find,
No peaceful end, for only to hold, only darkness,
Which now unfolds.

Death surrounds me, for it is time, and yet, I know,
For this I cry. Time has left me, I stand alone, within
The shadows, where I shall roam.

Beauty of the scenes now gone, before my eyes,
Which cannot see, the beauty gone, no longer there,
For only darkness, is what I share.

What is this? In dead man's eyes, but a distant, shed
Of light! Coming forth, to claim the soul, which lies alone,
Amongst the stone. Glory to the King above, for I leave,
Because of love. He who died in pain and grief, now awaits
At heaven's gate.

Into the light, of heaven's gate, my Master calls, for tis' my faith,
To bow, and praise, my Saviour's name, for He alone, has saved
This soul, from the fear, within the stone.

GERALD A. GOTT
30 October 1998

MISTY EYES

Misty eyes which never dry, because of
Pain, they seek to hide. Peering out, from
Sullen shame, to see the day, has brought
The rain.

Through the lonely, trees of amber, lies the
Solemn souls, which clamor. Among the moisten
Evergreens, never more, to search the sea.

Of the guilt, like darken skies, always there, before
My eyes. For I cry, beneath my breath, like the haunting,
Sound of death.

Weakness taketh, soul and all, for the sound, I hear
Has called, come before the darken tombs, for they
Are here, in each their room.

In the darkness, I stand and peer, for the sound, has
Brought me fear. Suddenly, without a sound, I found
Myself, beyond the ground.

GERALD A. GOTT
28 November 1998

DEATH IS NEAR

New life found, for crystal skies, which
Bring the light, now shine upon and
Break the night.

Heavy burdens lifted off, the back of souls,
Which were once lost, because the Light, has
Taken all, the darkness from, the souls which
Called.

Blessings now with open eyes, flow before
The souls tonight. But, weary eyes which fail
To see, that death is near, beyond the trees.

Lurking just, beyond the soul, waits the one,
With eager eyes, to steal the truth, to give a lie,
For man himself, will fall again, and leave the
Truth, this very night.

Death is near, the soul tonight, because of sin,
Within the light, broken fellowship with God who
Saved, this soul which wondered, on this day.

Blessings of the One who's near, separated due to
Fear, from the soul, which took the lie, and left behind,
The grieving Light.

GERALD A. GOTT
19 February 2000

ASHES UPON STONE

Upone the bright and sunny skies, came the blight,
Of human kind, darken skies filled with blood, the
Pain of death, struck from above.

Within the rolls, of cold hard stones, lies the souls,
Which are deceased, upon the ground, the stones
Now stand, covered with, the blood of man.

For in the rolls, of lifeless stones, covered by the
Darken skies, only ashes of death itself, lies upon
The land so vast, no light can shine, for life has left.

Sounds of grief, which linger on, and never stop, broken
Hearts of deep despair, sunken down, beyond repair, seeking
Solace anywhere.

Sudden stillness, in the mist, searching life, for none exist,
Only ashes, of death atone, of lifeless souls, now left alone.

GERALD A. GOTT
24 September 2001

WHITE STONES

Rolls of stone, line the hills of no return, silent
Whispers heard no more, for the brave, lie just
Beneath, the rustling leaves, of yesterday.

Souls that wander, in silent sleep, for the pain
Now feels no rain. White in nature, stones of strength,
Never moving standing still, for all the brave ones,
Which have been killed.

For the loved ones, left behind, seeking solace, which
Cannot hide. Tears of sorrow, upon the ground, silently
Falling without a sound.

As the crowd leaves, with heads bowed down, broken
Hearted and painful frowns, seeking answers on their
Way, never knowing another day.

As the night falls, upon the hills, rolls of stones, ever
Standing, always still, never moving, upon
The hill.

GERALD A. GOTT
30 December 2013

TOMBSTONE

Alone I wait, for the day, that
Thy should visit, in rainy haze,
Comfort me, this I pray. Alone I've been,
For many years, listening for, a voice
So dear, hearing tender words of truth,
Comforting souls, which lie so mute.

As I lie, within this tomb, only silence
Screams in tune, hearing deftness beneath
The trees, if only, I could feel the breeze.
Knowing that, in death alone, forever gone,
Beneath the stone.

Silence with a whispering ear, can only wait,
With those so near. For in darkness, alone I
Wait, for in time, there are no days.

For my soul, has left this earth, far above
Within the clouds, I kneel with others, which
Surround, the King of glory, upon His throne,
Within the mist, that we are shown.

GERALD A. GOTT
23 October 2014

More poems to come...

About the Author

I have been married to my lovely wife Sandy for forty-eight years. I have three children (Michael, David, and Kristine) and I have four grandchildren (Abby, Scotty, Jacob, and Christopher).

I have been writing for twenty-three years, after I quit playing in my band. I considered myself a novice writer—and I am happy with that.

At sixteen, I joined the Army. Two years later I joined the Navy for four years and then the Air Force for an additional four years. I served during the Vietnam War and during that time received an honorable discharge and went to college.

I presently live in Lockhart, Texas as I like living in small towns. I love to garden and write poetry. I also love opera and classical music. I also love to teach the Bible.

I have contributed some of my poems to my brother's book, "Poetry of a Dysfunctional Family" and this is where I got the idea of writing my own book.

I hope you enjoy "One Soul."

Gerald A. Gott

Other Books by Gerald A. Gott

"Poetry of a Dysfunctional Family"

By Sammy Lee Gott, contributions by Gerald A. Gott

ISBN: 978-1-4834-4539-7 (paperback)

ISBN: 978-1-4834-4541-0 (hardcover)

ISBN: 978-1-4834-4540-3 (eBook)

Gerald's brother, Author Sammy Lee Gott, was one of four boys in a dysfunctional family, raised by alcoholics. Despite this difficult beginning, he survived and prospered. In Poetry of a Dysfunctional Family, Gott—with his brother Gerald—shares through his recollections and poetry an understanding of some of the factors that make a family dysfunctional and explores ways to break the generational cycle of abuse. He believes understanding is the key—knowing that the pain and stress from the abuse of childhood lasts far into adulthood and that God is the key ingredient needed for recovery. In these verses, Gott puts into words what needed to be said when he could not find the courage to speak. He also tells the love story that arose between an abused man and the woman who worked to understand and help heal him. In this collection, one man recalls his dysfunctional family and abusive childhood in prose and poetry, knowing that the healing process begins with love and ends with forgiveness.

Amazon Review:

Beautiful and engaging book about surviving and prospering after growing up in a dysfunctional family.

This book is half poetry and half narrative prose. It is told by two brothers, Sam and Gerry Gott. Sam is the primary author.

I'm very impressed by the style of the book, for it is an emotional and raw telling of events tempered with insightful moments that shaped the way these two brothers see the world today. It is about their life journeys. From poor to financially well off. From emotional broken to loved and centered. From a feeling of self doubt to one of self worth. From a non-spiritual beginning to finding Christ. From not knowing what good parents are to raising independent and well adjusted children that have a sense of what family is really about.

This book will make you think. It will also make you cry.

The brothers grew up in the early 1940s. Their father was some sort of military / CIA operative and kept moving the family around every few months. The mother was a homemaker (well, she lacked the skills to make a decent home by today's standards). Both were alcoholics, both were verbally abusive, and both didn't know how to love themselves, let alone their family.

The boys spent a lot of time at Boystown, which was a blessing. They also left home by 17 and joined the military.

The poems and prose talk about all aspects of life - what it was like moving around so much, a lack of schooling (because they kept moving), early childhood years when they thought no one understood or loved them, relationships with women, finding Christ, relationships with their children, work, military service, and growing older.

Most books about dysfunctional families spend most of the pages defining what one is, not showing you the emotional scars. Most authors of books involving dysfunctional families write about resenting the world, they want to explain why they are the way they are, or they want to spread negativism in their book. Not this one. You see the growth, the hope, and the resolution. The authors demonstrate their forgiveness and their ability to have moved on.

Absolutely beautiful.

A must read. :-)

Made in the USA
Columbia, SC
19 June 2023

18022164R00155